W9-APW-242

H·H·Richardson

H·H·Richardson

Architectural Forms for an American Society

James F. O'Gorman

The University of Chicago Press
Chicago and London

James F. O'Gorman is Grace Slack McNeil Professor of American art at Wellesley College.

The University of Chicago Press, Chicago 60637
The University of Chicago Press, Ltd., London

Printed in the United States of America

96 95 94 93 92 91 90 89 88 87 54321

Library of Congress Cataloging-in-Publication Data

O'Gorman, James F.
H. H. Richardson : architectural forms for an American society.

Bibliography: p.
Includes index.
1. Richardson, H. H. (Henry Hobson), 1838–1886—Criticism and interpretation. 2. Romanesque revival (Architecture) —United States. I. Richardson, H. H. (Henry Hobson), 1838–1886. II. Title.
NA737.R5O36 1987 720'.92'4 86-19223
ISBN 0-226-62069-7

To the memory of my beloved Sylvia

Contents

Illustrations

Preface

Richardson was the grand exteriorist.
Frank Lloyd Wright

This study of the contribution of H. H. Richardson to the architectural shaping of an American society is published to coincide with the sesquicentennial of his birth in 1838 and the centennial of his premature death in 1886. It is justified not only by the calendar, but by the need for a reassessment of his achievement in the light of existing knowledge.

There are already a number of books about the man and his work. Van Rensselaer's monograph of 1888 is basic: an indispensable account of the architect's career as it appeared to an astute contemporary critic. The half-centennial of his death saw the publication of Henry-Russell Hitchcock's fundamental study which placed the architect in the perspective of his own time and that of the author. My exhibition of selected drawings by Richardson and his office (1974) added information about his design method and details about a number of commissions, facts augmented by a host of subsequent articles by myself and others. Finally, in 1982 appeared J. K. Ochsner's exhaustive catalog of the architect's work, both built and unbuilt. Although new factual materials continue to surface, the record after a century and more would seem to be known in outline.

What I have attempted here is a concentrated interpretation of the architect's achievement in its larger dimensions, drawing upon the wealth of scholarship now available. The following chapters constitute a coherent thesis which focuses upon architecture as image, upon building form as an expression of social program. Given the richly varied approaches to the study of architecture and its history possible today, this might well appear to be a narrowly art-historical method—in the formal, stylistic sense—but it is my thesis that the *image* is precisely what H. H. consciously or unconsciously had uppermost in mind. I take my methodology from my subject, not from contemporary historiographical fashion. Frank Lloyd Wright's description of Richardson as "the grand exteriorist" was certainly intended to be ambivalent (see chapter 7), but it was also apt. Richardson was in the main content to rely upon conservative structural techniques and traditional (French) planning processes, but sought, according to my argument, an innovative expressive language of form based in part upon the European past but adapted to contemporary American society. Since that society was becoming diversified before his eyes, he had in fact to develop a variety of forms. He never defined such a program in writing, but there is ample circumstantial evidence, and the witness of the work itself, to support such a reading.

I hasten to add that my concentration upon Richardson as an "exteriorist," as creator of a formal imagery consonant with the society of his time, does not mean that I think of him as a limited designer, one who was incapable of shaping significant spaces as well as expressive masses. A visit to the interior of Trinity Church, to the restored Senate Chamber in Albany, to the living hall of the R. T. Paine house in Waltham, Massachusetts, to the courtyard of the Allegheny County Courthouse in Pittsburgh, or to any of his suburban libraries will demonstrate the totality of Richardson's architectural talent. These are more than serviceable, they are profoundly moving spaces. Yet, in historical terms, I believe his imagery to have been his greatest contribution, and so I have emphasized it in this study.

I hope to address an informed but not necessarily a specialized readership, and so I have eschewed that scholarly crutch, the footnote. Ochsner's catalog fully documents each of Richardson's commissions. I have tried in the text frequently to refer to the source of a specific fact, idea, or quotation, and I have included an extensive bibliography, chronologically arranged, which contains significant publications devoted in whole or in part to Richardson's work since the 1870s. The present volume is a summation of my previous scholarly publications on the architect. These are listed in the bibliography, to which the reader seeking documentation is directed.

I aim not to add to the parade of footnote-studded publications that have marked recent scholarship on this subject, not to continue "nibbling away at the great architect's career," as Andrew Saint labeled this labor in his review of Ochsner's catalog, but to embrace the meaning of Richardson's work as a whole. In viewing the totality, some of the details inevitably get lost. I have not produced another monograph, if by that we mean a discussion of every design in the oeuvre, but have concentrated, after an introduction to the man and his career (chapters 1–2) and a brief characterization of the place of Trinity in his achievement (chapter 3), upon four key building types (chapters 4–6). In the last chapter (7) I stress what I believe to be Richardson's most important influences upon the next generation of architects. In some instances an intense study of one building seemed sufficient to make my point; in others, an analysis of a series of designs seemed more appropriate. Hence, the apparent differences in treatment between chapters 3–4 and 5–6. Whatever the approach, however, my intention has been to bring into sharp focus what I think is important and (by slight or omission) unimportant in Richardson's historical contribution to American architecture. This is necessarily a personal interpretation, although it is one balanced by a quarter of a century of looking at, reading and writing about, and teaching devoted to the work of the architect, his contemporaries, and his followers.

The production of this book has taken more years than I care to remember, and in that time I have amassed profound debts to more friends and scholars than I care to or can recall. Yet there are a few special names that must be acknowledged here, and I happily list them with the understanding that they are not the only ones who contributed to the profile of Richardson's achievement sketched in the following pages, nor are they or anyone but me responsible for it. Some encouraged, some tried to dissuade, but I am alone accountable for the thesis presented here.

I want, above all, to thank the many fine teachers who have influenced my career, and especially James S. Ackerman, Ernest Allen Connally, John Coolidge, Walter L. Creese, William H. Jordy, Jr., Charles E. Peterson, and Buford Pickens.

Three readers urged me to brave publication: Cervin Robinson, Peter Fergusson, and William H. Pierson, Jr. I am grateful to them all, and especially to the latter, for contributions to my work that go far beyond mere encouragement.

Other Richardson scholars have helped, through their publications or private correspondence or conversation, and chief among them are Jeffrey Karl Ochsner, John Coolidge, Francis Kowsky, Jack Quinan, Richard Chafee, Margaret Henderson Floyd, Cynthia Zaitzevsky, William H. Jordy, Jr., and Larry Homolka. We all owe a fundamental debt to Henry-Russell Hitchcock.

Others who should also be mentioned are Jean Baer O'Gorman, Katherine Green Meyer, Elaine Harrington, Catherine Allen, and H. H. Richardson III.

H·H·Richardson

1 • *Life*

He could charm a bird out of a bush.
Charles A. Coolidge

Henry Hobson Richardson was born at Priestley Plantation on the Mississippi River in St. James Parish, Louisiana, on 29 September 1838, the oldest of several children of Henry Dickenson Richardson and Catherine Priestley. His father was a prosperous merchant with the firm of Hobson and Company, cotton brokers, his mother, the descendant of the eighteenth-century British scientist and religious dissenter, Joseph Priestley. It was a pedigree which the architect, his family, and his biographers have always mentioned with pride, but no one has ever asked in print why a descendant of the English "discoverer of oxygen" came to be born in the land of the pelican.

Joseph Priestley was forced to leave England for America in 1794 because of his dissenting religious and political views, which were altogether too liberal and too Francophile during a time when the British were resisting the impact of revolution across the Channel. After years of unrest, he and his family eventually settled in Northumberland, Pennsylvania, where he died in 1804. His third child and second son, William, was a restless soul, in and out of business in England and France. He became a tool of international politics when he was presented to the French National Assembly in June 1792 (fig. 1), an event which caused his father much embarrassment at home, and hastened his departure for the New World. William, too, eventually turned up in Northumberland, married, and did a little farming.

It is clear that William was what once would have been called the "black sheep" of the Priestley family. And perhaps a bit more. In April 1800 the *Reading* (Pennsylvania) *Weekly Advertiser* accused him of an attempt to poison the Priestley household by putting arsenic into the flour chest! His motive has never been explained. Although the edition of the *Advertiser* of 7 June carried letters from both father and son denying the allegation, William had already left Northumberland in shame. Joseph, paternal love only slightly shaken by the incident, paid off his errant son's debts, and wrote to a friend that he felt "more compassion than resentment on his account. He is gone to seek a settlement in the Western Territory, and I do not expect, or wish to see him any more; but I shall continue to write to him, and give him my best advice." The architect and his descendants' pride of

1. J. Sayers, *Monsieur Francois Introduces Master Pr***ly to the National Assembly.* Engraving, published by Thomas Cornell, 18 June 1792. The political cartoon features William Priestley, son of Joseph and grandfather of H. H. Richardson. (By permission of the Trustees of the British Museum.)

2. Oak Alley, St. James Parish, Louisiana, 1836–38. The plantation next to Priestley's where Richardson was born. (Photo by Jean Baer O'Gorman.)

ancestry was untarnished by knowledge of this dark deed, for this skeleton first came out of the historical closet in F. W. Gibb's biography of the scientist, published in 1965.

The result of William's murderous attempt upon his family drove him westward, to Louisiana, where he eventually became prosperous enough to own the plantation on which his daughter gave birth to the future architect. The Richardsons were New Orleans people, and Catherine, the birth approaching, was probably escaping the late-autumn heat of the city. The boy grew up in one of the "Thirteen Sisters," a row of late Federal-style brick townhouses on Julia Street in the heart of the best residential district of the new American section of the city, but accompanied the family out to the bank of the river during the summertime. Priestley's was a west-bank plantation lying just south of Roman's, whose great house, Oak Alley, a building barely finished as Richardson breathed his first, is extant (fig. 2). The mature architect certainly recalled the shape of that or innumerable other houses along the river road, when, for very different types of buildings in a very different part of the country, he created simple forms dominated by all-embracing hip roofs (see fig. 69).

H. H., or "Fez," as he was known to his family for reasons still unexplained, emerges as a distinct personality at the age of fifteen, in May 1854. His father wanted then, through Senator Judah P. Benjamin, to enroll him at West Point, a wish that went unfulfilled.

The boy was a rather stumpy five feet tall, of sound constitution, of "the nervous bilious temperament," with dark hair and eyes, "spirited expression," ambitious of distinction, steady, persevering, generous, and courageous, or so thought the principal of the Classical Academy in New Orleans, which he had been attending since the age of nine. There he studied primarily the classics and mathematics, in which subject he was considered "the most promising pupil" the principal had ever taught. We also know he practiced French, music, horsemanship, and chess. Despite the same recommender's statement that no physical defect would impair his qualifications, the architect's first biographer, Van Rensselaer, attributed his failure to get into the military academy to a speech impediment, an affliction which, incidentally, handicapped his maternal great-grandfather as well. In later years H. H.'s pattern of speech was described as a series of explosions by one client, as "stutters and sputters" by another.

After a year treading water at Tulane University, the seventeen-year-old student journeyed to New England, where, after some cramming with Cambridge tutors, he was admitted to the freshman class at Harvard College in February 1856. Harvard in the 1850s was more the finishing school for Boston Brahmins than the academically distinguished graduate institution it has become in our century. Nothing in the record suggests that H. H. made his mark academically, despite the fact that his main subjects were the familiar classics and mathematics. Nor did his piety recommend him: between January and June 1859, as John Coolidge has pointed out, our undergraduate was cited forty times for missing chapel!

Although we know he never took a book out of the college library during his undergraduate years, he did read. Or, at least, he bought books from Ticknor and Field's Old Corner Book Store at Washington and School streets in the center of Boston. During the months he crammed the classics to pass the entrance to Harvard, that is, in the fall of 1855, he purchased Homer's *Odyssey*. Upon admission he shifted to history, Macaulay's of England and W. H. Prescott's of the reign of Philip II of Spain, but soon succumbed to the allure of romantic fiction, blowing $37.50 for Scott's Waverly novels, then moving on to such popular illustrated literature as Charles Lever's *Charles O'Malley* and Henry Cockton's *Valentine Vox, the Ventriloquist*. In his junior year he purchased the poetry of Burns and Wordsworth. Only one item shows an artistic taste, and that a decidedly popular one. In November 1857 he paid $24 for a handsome volume of engravings after the paintings of David Wilkie, an English follower of the

3. H. H. Richardson at Harvard College, 1859. (Courtesy of the Harvard University Archives.)

Dutch genre tradition. Such a list suggests a fashionable but not a distinctive cultivation.

In his *Education,* Henry Adams pinpointed the advantage of a Harvard sojourn during these years. "A student like H. H. Richardson, who came from far away New Orleans, and had his career before him to chase, rather than to guide[,] might make valuable friendships at college," he wrote. An affable fellow, darkly handsome (fig. 3), "full of creole life and animation," "vivacious and sympathetic in manner, forcible and amusing in conversation, clever, ardent," "generous to a fault," and possessed of a distinguished pedigree, Richardson slipped easily into the social life of social Harvard. It was later said of him, when talk turned to his way with clients, that "he could charm a bird out of a bush"; it was a talent undoubtedly developed at college, where he first met so many of these future accounts.

Our next sustained description of H. H. comes, in fact, from a fraternal setting (fig. 4). As an undergraduate he joined the Hasty Pudding, the Porcellian, and the Pierian Sodality. The last was a musical club for which he performed on the flute, an instrument he had studied in the south. He was initiated into the Pierian on 5 March 1857, after which the brotherhood repaired to Boston's famed Parker House. "Abounding in everything that the most fastidious Pierian

4. Winslow Homer, "The Junior Class at Harvard College." A generalized characterization of Richardson's clubby classmates. (*Harper's Weekly,* 1 August 1857.)

could ask and unsparingly moistened with Parker's choicest brand of wine, we do not hesitate to say that the Sodality has never seen a better supper," according to the club's records. The scribe, James A. Rumrill, who was to be instrumental in securing H. H. his first building, goes on to assure us that it could not have been otherwise "with so notorious a connoisseur as Mr. R. to do the polite. His generous hospitality has long ago secured him the name of a jolly good fellow." It is perhaps safe to hazard the guess that the principal of the Classical School in New Orleans had not thought of his charge's generosity as shining in such a jovial milieu. This is but the earliest account we have of Richardson presiding at a groaning board surrounded by good fellows. It was to become a characteristic vignette.

The very day H. H. was thus developing his future clientele for an as yet undefined career, his stepfather (his father having died in 1854) was writing a letter to James Walker, president of the college, which provides us with a second characteristic vignette. John Bein complains to the president that the boy's mother, Catherine, has not received a letter in more than three months, and what is worse, he is spending too much money, not on drinking and gambling, but a "very great extravagance in dress is one of the causes, and . . . horses is another." Although betting on the ponies does not appear among the grown man's weaknesses, it must be recorded that Richardson was ever a clothes-horse. At college, according to his brother, his "mock part" was "Nothing to Wear," a nickname probably derived from a humorous poem of that name published anonymously (but apparently written by William Allen Butler) in 1857 with illustrations by Augustus Hoppin. The little book chides the ladies with spending great fortunes on clothes but still having nothing to wear. It contains a "portrait" of the narrator that may be a reflection of the way H. H.'s classmates viewed him (fig. 5). This concern for dress remained with the architect, who died insolvent, in debt to, among many others, Poole's of London, the fashionable Savile Row tailors, for £53 14*s*. 6*d*. In this as in so much else, H. H. proved himself a worthy predecessor to Frank Lloyd Wright, among whose many axioms was something like this: Take care of the luxuries, the necessities will take care of themselves.

5. Augustus Hoppin, the Narrator, *Nothing to Wear,* 1857. The title of this popular poem, plus this "portrait" of the foppish narrator, may have suggested Richardson's college nickname. (Author's collection.)

James Rumrill's notes on the activities of the Pierian Sodality not only immortalize Richardson's joviality during his college days, they record for all history that he had, by May 1857, come under "feminine influence." It is not until February 1859 that we learn the identity of this influence as Julia G. Hayden, daughter of Dr. John Cole Hayden of Boston. It was an attachment that strengthened his ties to New England, for it was to Julia that he was to voice his anguish over his divided loyalities during the Civil War. And it was she, who stood by him in that conflict, who was to marry him at the outset of his professional career.

We still seek the exact moment when clubby "Fez" decided to study architecture. He came north intending to be a civil engineer, and we can suggest that his mathematical skills could have attracted him to the active architectural scene that was Boston-Cambridge during the 1850s. At Harvard, Boylston Hall (fig. 6) and the Chapel were under construction during his undergraduate years; downtown there was a host of recent, new, and rising works (see fig. 44). These were the products of various designers (Paul Schulze at Harvard;

6. Paul Schulze, Boylston Hall, Harvard College, 1857–58. Altered. (Courtesy of the Harvard University Archives.)

Gridley J. F. Bryant and partners in Boston), and they took on a variety of shapes in response to a variety of needs, but they shared a common and dominating characteristic. Many of the new buildings carried on the Boston tradition of granite design initiated by Bulfinch and his successor, Alexander Parris, in the 1810s and 1820s. Whether smooth or dressed, the granite block formed the basic unit of design, and its toughness dictated a minimum of ornament and a simple exterior form. Buildings arose that owed their presence to the most elemental of architectural characteristics: the contrast of textures, the simplicity of uprights and horizontals, often massive monoliths, the monochromatic result of gray stone upon gray stone, the economical hip-roofed parallelepiped. We can deduce from Richardson's mature work that he looked carefully at these buildings at some time during his life (see chapter 4); why not during his Cambridge undergraduate days when his eyes first opened to the art of architecture?

John Bein, who married his partner's widow in 1857, thus becoming Richardson's stepfather, deserves an honored niche in the history of American architecture, because it was he who made it possible, at some sacrifice to himself, for H. H. to mature within the Parisian architectural environment. During Richardson's last semester at Cambridge, when he was busy with whatever he did while skipping chapel, his stepfather wrote him from New Orleans (February 1859) that "a good Architect, if he is industrious, Cannot help but Succeed, & in order before you come out to New Orleans to pursue the Architectural business, I have thought that Six or Nine Months in London & Paris, where you will have full scope for your Instruments in Drawing, will do you more good than three times the time spent in N.O.." Bein begins his letter as many of us frequently do, apologizing for not writing for some time, which suggests that Richardson had written about an interest in architecture as a profession during the fall of 1858, about the time Paul Schulze finished Boylston Hall at the college. Be that as it may, Bein, himself no less generous than his stepson, offered to send H. H. abroad in June, despite the fact that he has "had to Struggle in business for the last Two years, & the very large am[oun]t I have lost, & I am still behind hand." He knows Catherine's son will not abuse the confidence placed in him, and H. H. did not, as six to nine months stretched into six and more years.

Richardson crossed the Atlantic in the summer of 1859 in the company of two classmates, one of whom was James Rumrill. After a tour of England, Scotland, and Ireland, he moved on to Paris where by the middle of September he had enrolled in the architectural

7. H. H. Richardson, drawing of part of the Ildefonso Group (now in the Prado, Madrid) 1860, after a cast in the Ecole des Beaux-Arts, Paris. (By permission of Mrs. Julian H. Richardson; courtesy of Shepley Bulfinch Richardson and Abbott, architects.)

atelier of Jules André in preparation for entrance into the Ecole des Beaux-Arts on the rue Bonaparte. We assume he chose Paris over London for his architectural education because of his francophile New Orleans background. The Ecole was free, open to anyone, Frenchman or foreigner, between fifteen and thirty years old, who could pass the entrance examinations, which were, of course, given entirely in French. Richardson failed to gain admission that fall, but was admitted the next, on 20 November 1860, by placing eighteenth in a field of 120. Once admitted, he attended as did all the students, optional lectures in theory, history, structure, and related subjects at the Ecole itself, and he also worked on one or more required problems in design or construction (*concours*) per year under the general supervision of the patron of his atelier or its older members. Over the next four years and more, as Richard Chafee has shown, Richardson participated in a great number of *concours,* establishing during his stay there a record of achievement judged good by comparison with his fellow students. Although almost nothing survives of the work he executed at the Ecole, we know he studied structure and design, drew from antique casts (fig. 7), and even painted.

At Paris as at Cambridge H. H. made friends easily. There exists a familiar description of him as "an excellent companion, but though fond of pleasure and society and always ready for a dinner-party or a dancing-party, he never allowed these things to interfere with the serious performance of his work. . . . [He was] a slender youth of promising talent, a good-tempered and amiable companion." In addition to Henry Adams, who occasionally popped over from London where he served as secretary to his father, the wartime ambassador, Richardson's Parisian friends included two atelier mates and future coveted Prix-de-Rome winners, Adolphe Gerhardt and Julien Guadet, as well as the Englishmen R. Phené Spiers. They were to become major architects or educators in the coming years, and all maintained an association with their American peer.

Except for Richardson's southern roots, it might have been an idyllic way to spend the war years. Union soldiers under command of Major-General Benjamin F. Butler of Massachusetts entered the city of New Orleans on 1 May 1862. Two weeks later Richardson wrote to Julia Hayden that "New Orleans is taken—governed by strangers. . . . I burned with shame when I read [of] the capture of my city and I in Paris." Burned with shame, and frustration, for H. H. was trapped squarely between his youth and family in the South, and his friends and future in the North. The dilemma had already driven him back to Boston in October 1861, perhaps in company with Henry

Adams, who wrote that "Richardson . . . was in a horrible position. His family and property are in New Orleans. He is himself a good Union man, I believe . . . but he does not want to do anything which will separate him from his family or make them his enemies. . . . I strongly advised him not to think of ever living in New Orleans again; at least not as an architect."

Richardson landed in Boston on 17 October. There he was immediately confronted with the quandary of his position: in the North he was an enemy alien since, out of consideration for his family, he refused to take an oath of allegiance to the Union. Thought of returning to the South was discouraged on all sides by his northern friends, who agreed with Adams that it would damage his career. A retreat to Europe seemed the only possible action. After a winter of discontent he was back in Paris by mid-March 1862, from which neutral place he wrote a series of letters to Julia. "Politics I wash my hands of, externally at least," he reported at the end of the month. But the price of outward composure was an internal struggle of which we have only occasional glimpses and will never fully fathom. It is clear that events in Louisiana struck hard. On 17 April he wrote that "operations have been commenced against New Orleans. I feel nervous and anxious to hear more. My poor mother and sisters—if I thought I could in any way aid them . . . I would go tomorrow." By mid-May, as we have seen, he knew his native city was under the fist of "Beast" Butler and his troops.

Richardson's financial condition worsened first with the northern blockade of the South in April 1861, and finally with the fall of New Orleans in May 1862. By the end of that month he had made up his mind to go to work, at least part-time. By mid-summer H. H. was drafting in the offices of Théodore Labrouste, himself a Rome Prize winner and older brother of the more famous Henri, and J. I. Hittorf, and writing chatty letters to Julia about his busy schedule at work and at school. He continued despite his need to earn his keep to take an active part at the Ecole, both as to executing *concours* and participating in school politics to the degree that a foreigner could. As David Van Zanten has written, the 1860s on the rue Bonaparte was a "tumultuous and fruitful decade." A clash of ideologies between traditional Ecole classicists and outside but powerfully backed Gothicists led to a decree by Napoleon III dated 13 November 1863 which sought to reform the governance of the school and place, among others, E. E. Viollet-le-Duc, the French theoretician and practitioner of the Gothic Revival, on the faculty. Viollet's lectures between January and March 1864 led to repeated student rioting which finally forced his resignation. Richardson, never an admirer of Viollet, took part in at least one of these demonstrations, in consequence of which, and of his appearance, given "by good clothes from Poole's" as he himself explained, had the good fortune of spending a sociable night in jail with Théophile Gautier, author, among a vast number of other writings, of the *Histoire du romantisme*.

The end of the war brought an end to Richardson's stay in Paris. Despite pleas from his family that he return to New Orleans, he sailed in October 1865 for the North. We will probably never know what pain that decision cost him, but having made it, he never looked back. He never returned to the South, and eventually found it possible to design Union military memorials as well as buildings for friends and clients who had served with the northern forces. As Phillips Brooks later put it so simply, "the war was over, and there was work to do."

That work appeared more promising in New York than in Boston; at least Richardson originally sought to establish himself on the Hudson rather than the Charles. His first situation was in Brooklyn with a builder named Roberts whom he had met in Paris. There turned out to be a "complete want of sympathy" between the two, according to Richardson, and they parted company as "good friends" in April 1866. He wrote his brother, William, that he was "prepared for a hard time for some months but have confidence in ultimate success. All I want now is an order."

He was at this time "of good height, broad-shouldered, full-chested, dark complexion, brown eyes, dark hair parted in the centre . . . he wore his clothes . . . with an indescribable air of ease. . . . His shoes were thick, broad-soled, and looked more as if made in England than in France." He preferred to speak French to English, according to one who shared a Brooklyn boarding house with him, although he spoke either with a stammer. He seemed, however, otherwise fit, and given to taking cold baths in the morning and long walks between bouts of study among the architectural books he had brought with him from Paris.

He had little else to do, for these were dark days of waiting, and lack of work meant little money but much time. He did not, however, present the appearance of poverty. What his later friend and collaborator, Frederick Law Olmsted, was to call after his death "his characteristic, unconquerable recklessness in personal [financial] matters," about which his stepfather had once complained to President Walker of Harvard College, is illustrated in these days by a story told by his boarding-house companion that, on his way to the Century Club one evening, he paused to call attention to his state. "Look at me," he said, "I wear a suit made by Poole, of London, which a nobleman might be pleased to wear, and—and—and I haven't a dollar to my name." Richardson had indeed stopped by Poole's on his way home from Paris in October 1865 to purchase nearly thirty-seven pounds' worth of apparel.

His companion thought the finery covered a state of despondency about his prospects, and grief at the death of his mother in far-off New Orleans. The pall lasted a short six months, however, for early in November 1866 H. H. received his first independent commission, the design for the Church of the Unity at Springfield, Massachusetts (see fig. 17). It was an award he owed as much to his friendship with James Rumrill as to the intrinsic merits of his proposal. The influence of his former Cambridge associates continued to shape his career as his ability to create the "bold, rich, living architecture" he believed in from the beginning became more mature. With the Church of the Unity Richardson was off and running; it was the order he had wished for in his letter to his brother of the previous spring.

His career launched, marriage became possible. Julia and Hal, as she called him, were joined in Cambridge early in January, and stopped at the Rumrill's in Springfield on their wedding trip back to New York. Richardson had already switched from the Brooklyn boarding house to a rented cottage on Staten Island. Just two years later the Richardsons moved again with their first child, Julia Hayden, born in 1867, into the new house at Clifton, Staten Island, designed by H. H. and paid for, perhaps somewhat reluctantly, by his father-in-law (fig. 8). John Cole Hayden wrote to his wife in April 1869 that the "building of the house was premature and a mistake decidedly—it cost too much—it worries him very much." And it remained another debt unretired at the architect's death in 1886, nearly two decades later. In that mortgaged cottage H. H. and his family lived until he moved back to the Boston area in 1874, and there the next four children were born: John Cole Hayden (named after his maternal grandfather) in 1869, Mary Houghton in 1871, Henry Hyslop in 1872, and Philip in 1874. (Frederick Leopold William arrived in Brookline in 1876; he was named for the client and two associates of his father at the State House in Albany, then under construction.) Julia Hayden Richardson, who survived her husband by many years, proved to be a constant companion to the architect. Olmsted described her at the time of H. H.'s death as "an admirable woman of child-like simplicity, strong, brave, efficient. He could not have been happier in a wife." On Staten Island and later in Brookline, Olmsted was a neighbor of the Richardsons, and he remembered Julia as "among the kindest of friends."

Richardson lived on Staten Island, but his office was in Manhattan, to which he commuted by boat. At first he shared space in the Trinity Building on Broadway with the architect E. J. Little, but on 1 October 1867 he formed a limited partnership with Charles Dexter Gambrill with offices at 6 Hanover Street and later at 57 Broadway. The association lasted until 1878 (two years before Gambrill's suicide), but it was more of convenience than of collaboration. Nonetheless, the works of the late sixties and early seventies bear the name of the partnership.

In New York, Richardson built the foundations of his architectural career. While Julia tended the children on the island, the architect ferried, when healthy enough, across the river each morning to his office in Manhattan. Why Richardson chose thus to commence

8. H. H. Richardson, the architect's first house, Staten Island, New York, 1868–69. Altered. (Courtesy of the Staten Island Historical Society.)

his career remains an unanswered question, an especially perplexing one in light of the fact that the buildings which grew under his Hanover Street pencil were primarily destined for upstate New York or New England. Between November of 1866 and the spring of 1874, when he removed his family to Massachusetts, Richardson designed some forty-four buildings and projects, only nine of which were located in New York City (and many of these were minor alterations), six were for locations unknown, and three were for elsewhere (including one for Argentina). Could New York have been a place to cool off after the passions of the Civil War, which Boston had done so much to ignite? It must have been clear to all that Richardson's future, his professional career, and his personal relationships demanded relocation to the Boston area. The only question was when.

From 1869 until 1876 the architect kept at his elbow a large sketchbook in which he not only recorded preliminary ideas for many of these early projects but occasionally jotted down personal notes as well. Thus, on 30 September 1872, thirty-four years and one day after his birth and the day his fourth child and second son was born, he drafted a list of clothes for John Cole Hayden, his first son, as if he had been about to order the three-year-old's wardrobe from Poole's. It included a suit consisting of jacket, waistcoat, and kilt, an overcoat, and white shirts. He also mused about his growing family, listing the children's initials opposite those of the parents. He showed himself no better or worse than most Victorian fathers by beginning with the initials of his two sons, who were in fact the second and fourth in order of birth, and following with those of his daughters, who were first and third. The psychologist might make an issue of that, and more of the facts that we know something about the eldest son from the father, but nothing about the father from the eldest son, and that we know something about the father from the eldest daughter, but nothing about her from him. This might just reflect the preoccupation or neglect of a busy man, but Richardson was remembered by his family and others as a "man's man," and the description seems to apply indoors as well as out.

These genealogical notes of 30 September 1872 occur on a page which includes several rough sketches for an unidentified house. Could the architect have been counting his brood and wondering if his present coop ought to be replaced by a larger one? And where, indeed, might that larger one be located? Four months earlier he had won the competition for the design of Trinity Church, Boston, and it must have become apparent then, if not before, that his exile on the Hudson was nearing an end. Which it did, in the spring of 1874.

The Richardsons moved not to Boston or to Cambridge but to Brookline. The choice was no accident. That area of the Boston suburbs lying just west of Jamaica Pond was in the nineteenth century, as it remains today, a landscape of rolling hills dotted with large houses inhabited by men of wealth, achievement, and influence. Described as a "wealthy and beautiful suburban town" in a Massachusetts gazetteer published the year of the architect's move, Brookline by 1888 could be characterized as a place which "has long enjoyed the preeminent reputation of being the wealthiest in the United States." Other areas might dispute such a sweeping claim, but mature affluence did make for social self-assurance. Brookline is the location of the first country club in the United States, called to this day simply The Country Club. It was founded in 1882.

The undulating land west of Jamaica Pond had long appealed to residents and visitors alike because of its parklike apperance. The landscape architect and author Andrew Jackson Downing wrote in 1840 that "this neighborhood . . . is a kind of landscape garden, and there is nothing in America . . . so inexpressibly charming as the lanes which lead from one cottage, or villa, to another. . . . [The] tempting vistas and glimpses under the pendant boughs give it quite an Arcadian air of rural freedom and enjoyment." These lines were echoed by Van Rensselaer in her biography of the architect when she wrote that "Brookline's site was naturally picturesque—richly wooded, everywhere rolling, in some parts really hilly, and often boldly broken by huge grey ledges of rock. Thus every place has personality, . . . but the most beautiful and most interesting of all is Mr. Sargent's."

Charles Sprague Sargent, Harvard graduate, dendrologist, and first director of the Arnold Arboretum, was one of the large number of prominent men who lived in south Brookline after the Civil War. All lived within a short walk of Holm Lea, the Sargent estate. All lived in the comfortable, large, stone or frame houses which crown the hills or nestle in the valleys of this garden suburb. Such a suburb was an ideal location for a young and coming architect with professional and social ambitions for himself and his family. As Richardson's erstwhile architectural associate, P. B. Wight, wrote at the time of H. H.'s death, the architect chose to live in Brookline "where he was surrounded by the friends of his wife and the refined and cultured society whose association and sympathy he craved." For Richardson, Brookline was the right address.

Sargent's Holm Lea was bordered on the south by Cottage Street, one of Downing's picturesque lanes rising sinuously from Ja-

9. Samuel Gardner Perkins house, Cottage Street, Brookline, Massachusetts, 1803. (Photo by the author.)

maica Pond to Warren Street. Across Cottage near Warren stands the Samuel Gardner Perkins house, erected in 1803 (fig. 9). A cruciform, framed, two-story structure with elongated service wing stretching to the rear, the house looks out through a portico of widely spaced, slender piers supporting a low hip roof. It is similar to a number of porticoed Federal farm houses in the area, but Richardson's successor, Charles A. Coolidge, probably reflected the architect's own thoughts when he saw it, for Coolidge later wrote that it was "built in the style of the planters' houses in the South." In a vague way the Perkins house must have reminded Richardson of his lost youth, of his summers spent in the shadows of the great peripteral houses of the river road out of New Orleans (see fig. 2).

Since 1864 the Perkins house had been the property of Edward William ("Ned") Hooper, a Harvard classmate and one of Richardson's closest friends. Ned Hooper rented the place to the architect in the spring of 1874, and for the next twelve years Cottage Street hummed with architectural activity. At first H. H. worked out of the front portion of the first floor, but as business increased he began to expand his workspace through a series of sheds extending out into the two-acre plot. By the time of his death these sheds, or "Coops" as they came to be called, consisted of two ranges of separate drafting alcoves and common office area stretching from the dwelling to an enclosed, fireproof, masonry structure housing the architect's library and study (fig. 10). Here was assembled the rich assortment of architectural publications and objets d'art collected by the architect during his travels abroad. One draftsman described the room in part as a "dreamland beyond" in which "a hugh center table was fitted with the rarest volumes, brick-a-brac and choice bits generally; bookcases and sconces ranged along the walls; casts and vases showed off beautifully in the subdued light against deep maroon walls; the solid gold ceiling, with its great, sturdy oak beams, from which were suspended

10. H. H. Richardson's library, Cottage Street, Brookline. Demolished. (After Van Rensselaer, *Henry Hobson Richardson and His Works*, 1888.)

here and there all varieties of oriental lamps of the most intricate metal workmanship—all were overpowering. . . . This room was a magic source of inspiration, and in the long winter months it was the retreat for all during noon hours." Although there was hope at the architect's death that the ensemble might be preserved, it and the Coops were leveled when his successors, Shepley, Rutan, and Coolidge, moved the business into the center of Boston, and the room's contents were dispersed to settle claims on his insolvent estate.

To these Coops and this library Richardson brought his draftsmen, who were in reality his students. He created in Brookline a home-studio somewhat on the model of the French atelier. His office became a kind of finishing school for students from the Massachusetts Institute of Technology, who vied for the honor and the rewards of working for him. They formed part of an extended family group that included the architect's wife and children. As Van Rensselaer wrote, "the life of the home and the life of the office went on together. . . . The elder students were constantly at his hearth and table and seemed as much a part of his family as the children whom he loved to have about him while at work and to take with him on hurried business journeys."

In Brookline Richardson carried on the good fellowship that had marked his days at Harvard and in Paris. Sunday afternoons were given over to musical receptions where visitors, some from abroad, could enjoy chamber music by Haydn or Cherubini while viewing drawings of the architect's latest projects. On Monday evenings he gathered around his board present and former students. He joined groups devoted to the enjoyment of the culinary arts, including the famed Saturday Club and the Wintersnight. Charles Coolidge recalled one menu for the latter, when Richardson called it to order around the specially constructed black oak table in his red-walled dining room: "the wines came from old cellers in New Orleans, the oysters from Baltimore, and the terrapin from Augustin's famous Philadelphia restaurant, with a chef in attendance all the way." And the conversation was as good as the cuisine.

Richardson was a passionate architect, a jolly host, and a fond father. His oldest child, Julia, remembered that all of his offspring thought that they shared in his work. At table an idea would spring to mind and he would send them flying for pencil and paper, "and as we hung over him he consulted us as to doors and windows." Julia was her father's frequent companion "when he drove his pair of fine horses in a goddard buggy to inspect his buildings in Cambridge and

Boston. He always had some of us children with him and we revelled in it, he was so gay and full of fun." When separated from them he thought of them often, as his letters from Europe during the summer of 1882 bear witness.

During his last winter, while he was busily and wearily trying to keep up with work that stretched from Washington to St. Louis and Chicago, he found time to write several preserved letters to his eldest son, letters filled with the kind of paternal advice that bores children and frustrates unheeded adults. In one, dated October 1885, father writes to son that he thought the son's last letter good "because it was natural bordering as it does on impudence and conceit." Hayden had had some cards printed, adding Mr. to his name. Father disapproves of a sixteen-year-old using a man's title, and asks him to destroy the lot. He also has reservations about Hayden's accepting an invitation to visit the Marshall Fields in Chicago. But he looks forward to returning to Brookline so he can go shooting with the boy. Finally, he orders Saturday supper. He wants four courses: "plain" oyster soup, lobster *en coquille,* roast duck, and mushrooms on toast.

Hayden did visit the Marshall Fields at their mansarded Prairie Avenue house in Chicago on the occasion of the famous Mikado Ball held for their children at New Year's, 1886. Father sent this advice following after: "Keep your bowls open, your teeth white, & never forget that you are a guest. . . . Don't leave family letters lying around loose servants are fond of prying. . . . Be polite & cordial even, if you choose, but familiar with no one. Don't laugh too loud nor immoderately. Get all the sleep you can." It was the same kind of tiresome advice that fathers have been sending to sons from time immemorial, the same tiresome advice generated by paternal love and concern. It was, as with so much in family relationships, boring, necessary, and touching. There is no reason to believe that H. H. was other than a devoted husband and dedicated father.

Other late letters display the fusion of family and business in the architect's Brookline existence. During early February 1886 Julia Richardson visited Washington with her oldest daughter, apparently for her health. In one letter from Brookline, Richardson is solicitous of her and eager for news of his work under construction there, all in the same breath: "Wear two undershirts if the weather is extreme. . . . Don't fail to see the Anderson's house. . . . Write me about the Hay house. . . . Tell Henry [Adams] I am making a wrought iron & plate glass screen for his study mantel." The next day he writes surrounded by his children, happy to have received letters from his daughter but unhappy with their content. "Why dont somebody write me about the Hay house & the Anderson house. I am longing to hear what you think of them. Dont come home on Saturday . . . I really think you ought to get thoroughly well before coming back otherwise all will be thrown away as much as I want you & as much as I suppose you want to get back I beg you not to hurry that is if you feel that you are improving & having a good time." The run-on prose suggests the passion of a man filled with vitality. The facts were otherwise.

The second half of the letter just quoted is filled with ominous news about H. H.'s health. It was an all too familiar topic for his family. From the beginning of his career Richardson had labored in poor health. The drawings for Trinity Church, his first great work, were made in bed in the house on Staten Island. Throughout his life his letters to family, friends, and business associates were filled with complaints from water on the knee to hernias and beyond. The proximity of family and work in the Brookline establishment resulted largely from his medical needs. The maladies were many, but the central sickness, that which finally killed him, was nephritis or Bright's Disease, a chronic renal disorder. In his later years it began to control his life.

Richardson's "lightening" trip to Europe in the summer of 1882 was characteristically generated by work, pleasure, and sickness. In London he not only chatted with William Morris and Edward Burne-Jones and looked at the works of William Burges and Richard Norman Shaw, he was also examined by Sir William Gull of Guy's Hospital, the queen's physician and a world-renowned expert on renal disease. Gull's prognosis was guardedly optimistic, but he prescribed mainly moderation, of which the architect was completely incapable. From London H. H. journeyed to Paris, the south of France, the north of Italy, and Spain in search of his beloved Romanesque architecture, traveling at a breathtaking pace all the way. He returned to home and office in the fall, in the words of one client, "no better in health and even less capable of activity." In his last years he knew he was in a race against time, that death might still his drafting pencil at any moment, and with so much good work still to be done.

The winter of 1886 brought him finally to bed, flattened as much by a second hernia as by his nephritis. On the last day of 1885 he wrote to John Hay disclosing an accident that caused an "umbilical hernia, new species" which required a second truss. In the midst of this not dangerous but certainly alarming and tiresome affliction, Richardson's oft-noted wit and optimism shine through. "I am really now," he wrote to Hay, "what with my old and new ones, so covered and held together with pads, buckles, straps etc., that when I stretch real hard, I'm not quite certin that I'll come together in the same place again." But he was not always in a sunny mood, as the effects of his disease led to greater and greater debilitation. He was, during this time, according to another client with whom he stayed while in Washington on business, "a great deal of trouble. He bullies and nags everybody; makes great demands upon our time and service; must ride, even if he has to go but a square; gets up at noon; and has to have his meals sent to his room."

His problems were compounded by his girth. The "slender youth" of the Ecole des Beaux-Arts at the end weighed some 345 pounds. He was indeed a mountain of a man for the last four years of his life or, as another client put it, "a mournful object for size" (fig. 11). "I know you have no carriage strong enough to carry me from the depot," Richardson wrote to Henry Adams in July 1884, perhaps in jest but with grim reason as well. Heft was common among nineteenth-century gentlemen of comfort (H. H. with his two traveling companions to Europe in 1882 totaled over 900 pounds), but Richardson's weight was not caused by exaggerated intake alone. It was aggravated by the disease that killed him, on 27 April 1886, in the middle of his forty-eighth year.

Eulogies poured in, including the news that he had been nominated for the Gold Medal of the Royal Institute of British Architects, then a rare distinction for an American. Characteristic of the short-term reaction to his passing is the little-known statement of John Hay. Two days after Richardson's death Hay wrote to his widow that he had "lost in him one of the friends I most cherished and valued—and the loss to the country is irreparable . . . his place is assured as the first architect in our history and . . . [for] his friends his memory is enshrined as that of a pure and honorable gentlemen, of a temper as bright and genial as sunshine, with a mind and spirit both of extraordinary force and rectitude." The linking of personal and professional characteristics is common to these eulogies. "The man and his work are absolutely one" is the much reproduced observation of his friend, the Reverend Phillips Brooks.

Few dissenting voices are heard in the litany of contemporary descriptions of Richardson as a sympathetic personality, a man one would want to be with, although this may have been a masculine assessment. He was a "man's man," and Mrs. J. J. Glessner found him "aside from his profession . . . not what I should call an interesting man." Again, his identification with his profession is central, and indeed, his life is without meaning without the architecture he pro-

11. Hubert von Herkomer, *H. H. Richardson,* 1886. (Courtesy of H. H. Richardson III.)

duced. Richardson sought from the beginning, and with increasing urgency toward the end, to create a major reputation in his profession through the quality of his design. The enormous amount of literature devoted to that design that has appeared since his death (see Bibliography) attests to his accomplishment, but Richardson was lucky enough, despite his dying in mid-career, to see his efforts crowned with laurels during his lifetime. In 1885 the *American Architect and Building News,* the leading professional journal of the day, polled seventy-five architects to determine what they thought were the ten best buildings in the United States. Five of the ten selected by his peers were designed by Richardson, and the top of the list named Trinity Church, Boston (in 1956 a similar poll conducted by *Architectural Record* still ranked Trinity fourth out of fifty; in 1985 a poll of Fellows of the American Institute of Architects ranked it sixth of ten). But John Hay's description of Richardson as "the first architect in our country" suggests that contemporaries saw his achievement in terms of a framework larger than his own time. From his day to ours, Richardson's work has been recognized as distinctly different from anything America had produced before. This study attempts to identify what it was that set Richardson's work apart from its context, and what effect it had on the architectural shaping of an American society.

LYCEUM

2 • *Work*

The man and his work are absolutely one.
Phillips Brooks

H. H. Richardson's professional activities spanned a scant two decades, from his return to the United States after his study in Paris, in October 1865, until his middle-aged death at forty-seven, in April 1886. His architectural journey was relatively brief in time but long on achievement and influence. During these two decades he was to climb from well-connected obscurity to the pinnacle of his world, and from a derivative and often awkward eclecticism to an architecture of profound and powerful synthesis. But his path was neither direct nor simple, and any profile of his career must detail the periods of his development and recognize the variety of responses he generated in answer to the variety of design problems he confronted.

When Richardson arrived in New York in 1865, one of the most recent and important buildings in the city was the National Academy of Design (1861–65) by Peter B. Wight (who was later to be associated with Richardson in Chicago and write one of his most useful obituaries). Wight's now-demolished Academy building (fig. 12) was an early monument to the influence of John Ruskin in America. It was modeled after Ruskin's fa-

12. (*Left*) P. B. Wight, National Academy of Design, New York, 1861–65. Demolished. (Courtesy of the National Academy of Design, New York.)

13. Arthur Gilman and Gridley J. F. Bryant, City Hall, Boston, 1861–65. (Courtesy of the Bostonian Society, Old State House.)

vorite Venetian building, the Palazzo Ducale, and exemplified the Englishman's call for a vibrant nineteenth-century architecture based upon the medieval buildings of northern Italy. Alive with color, carved ornament, and Gothic details, the Academy represented one aspect of the derivative architectural situation at the end of the Civil War. When Richardson traveled to Boston that winter, as he certainly did to visit his fiancée, he would have seen there another recent building exemplifying a second aspect of contemporary style. This was Boston's new (now "old") City Hall (1861–65), designed by Arthur Gilman in association with Gridley J. F. Bryant (fig. 13). Like the Academy, City Hall reflected foreign influence, but, unlike the Academy, this influence was French. Gilman sought inspiration for his design in the pavilions, piled orders, and mansard roofs of the Second Empire as they were most impressively employed at the New Louvre in Paris. Although H. H. probably found City Hall somewhat skimpy by comparison to contemporary Parisian work, the Second Empire was to have a major influence on American public building, just as Ruskin's Victorian Gothic was to affect other types of postwar design.

The Academy and City Hall were significant, influential examples of the derivative state of American architecture that had existed since before the Revolution, and that entered a new phase with these works. American architects were on the receiving end of ideas generated in Europe, especially in England and France, and to a lesser extent in Germany. From the 1850s on, these ideas originated in the polychromatic, picturesque, medieval-based building of Victorian London, the academic classicism of Second Empire Paris, and the round-arched Romanesque (*Rundbogenstil*) of Munich and elsewhere in Germany. As exemplified in, say, George Gilbert Scott's St. Pancras Hotel (1868–74), High Victorian Gothic buildings were conglomerations of bits and pieces from the medieval past, the discrete parts assembled in disharmonic ways to produce asymmetrical, particolored dynamics (fig. 14). Jarring conjunctions, cacophonic

14. George Gilbert Scott, St. Pancras Hotel, London, 1868–74. (Photo by the author.)

15. Ludovico Visconti and Hector Lefuel, Pavillon Richelieu, New Louvre, Paris, 1852–57. (Photo by the author.)

clusterings, and vibrating colors, textures, shadow patterns, and natural ornament combine to create a dazzling package, restless, assertive, and filled with rich associations. As exemplified by the New Louvre of Ludovico Visconti and Hector Lefuel (1852–57), the Second Empire building was a measured range of floors interrupted at regular intervals by pavilions articulated by tiers of paired, freestanding columns and capped by high mansard roofs (fig. 15). The surfaces are monochromatic but thrown into high relief by the classical details and the rich sculptural embellishment. It was a robust three-dimensional architecture, although considerably less shrill than contemporary work across the Channel. As exemplified by Karl Schinkel's commercial or industrial work, or the buildings of the 1830s on the Ludwigstrasse in Munich by Friedrich von Gaertner, the *Rundbogenstil* combined elements of the classic and Romanesque to create masonry buildings of simple forms and repetitious round-arched details (fig. 16). Its influence was felt in America in the works of Paul Schulze at Harvard College in the 1850s (see fig. 6) as well as the mid-century Boston commercial work of Gridley J. F. Bryant (see fig. 44).

Like Peter Wight, Arthur Gilman, or Paul Schulze, most American architects of the postwar decades sought to adapt these European modes, more often than not working in all three styles as commissions warranted, and occasionally, as in the case of Philadelphia's Frank Furness, combining English and French sources into richly original eclectic patterns of their own (see fig. 36 and chapter 3). The Victorian Gothic lent itself to ecclesiastical, public, and memorial buildings; Second Empire classicism, to governmental and commercial structures; the *Rundbogenstil* to a spectrum of works from ecclesiastical to industrial. By the early 1870s, the American city began to reflect the influx of these mid-century foreign styles, as custom houses and post offices of modern French classicism replaced Greek Revival buildings from an earlier age, and Ruskinian Gothic churches sprouted side by side with older Georgian, Federal, or early Gothic

16. Frederich von Gaertner, Bayerische Berg- und Salzwerke, Munich, 1840–43. (Photo by the author.)

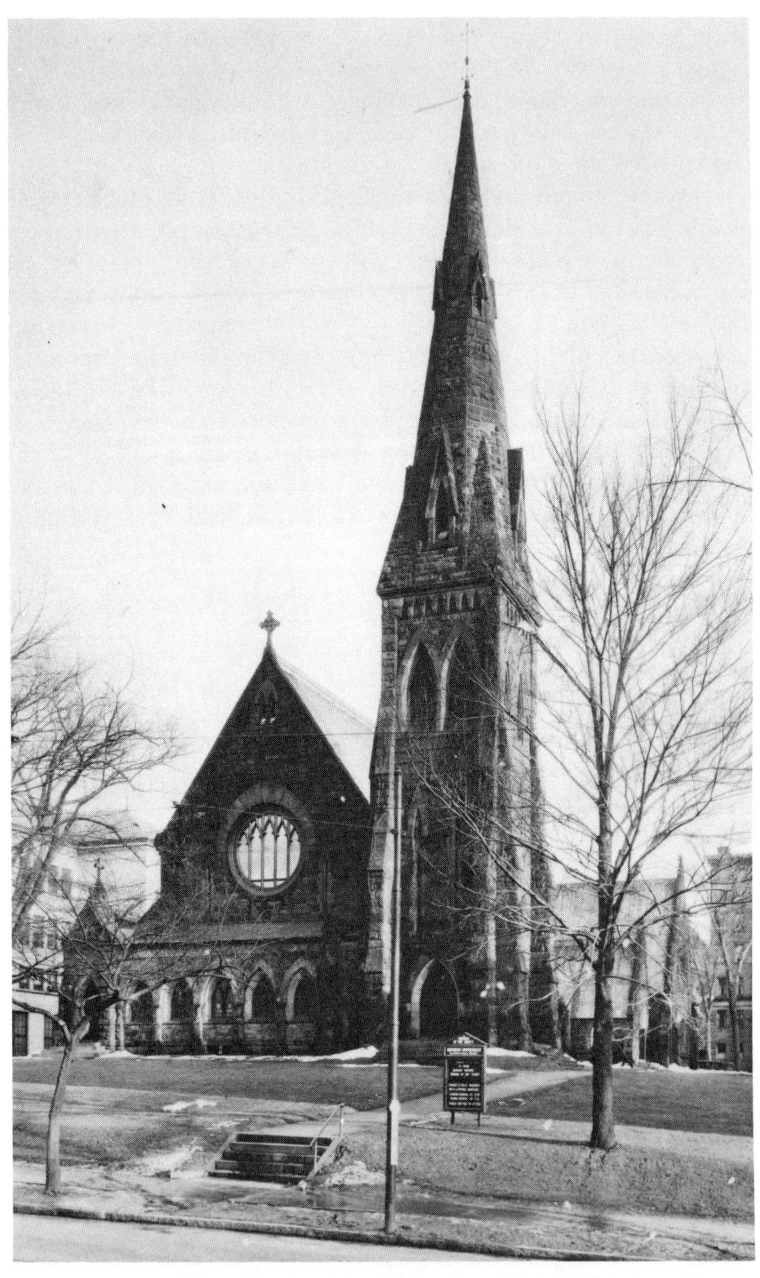

17. H. H. Richardson, Church of the Unity, Springfield, Massachusetts, 1866–69. Demolished. (Courtesy of the Springfield Public Library.)

Revival meeting houses. The Early Republican city was transformed during these decades, as the growing size and wealth of the nation necessitated larger and more imposing structures, and American architects sought guidance among the current fashions of the Continent.

Richardson was, of course, conversant with the latest English and French modes from his years abroad, and his growing architectural library reflected his early interest in continental styles. As a beginning practitioner, he could scarcely escape the influence of contemporary taste, and it is not surprising to find his early work a series of tentative essays in English and French style. This period of gestation lasted from his first work, the Church of the Unity in Springfield, Massachusetts (1866–69), until the early 1870s.

Unity (fig. 17), which was demolished about 1960, and a second work commissioned the following year, Grace Church in West Medford, Massachusetts (1867–69), take their stylistic cues from English ecclesiastical design, although it is true that similar French churches are not unknown, yet each is built of a local stone that gives it a particular flavor. Unity had three aisles and a clerestory, Grace has but one nave; both, however, were gabled structures animated by asymmetrical towers with broach spires. Contemporary descriptions call them Italian Gothic, but this seems only to suggest the Italian sources of High Victorian design. Each is a competent work, but neither is prophetic of the vitality to come.

English Gothic was the expected style of church architecture in the 1860s; for early residential designs, such as his own house on Staten Island (1868–69; see fig. 8), or that for William Dorsheimer in Buffalo (1868–71), Richardson turned to French sources. In his own house he merged the pavilion and mansard combination of the Second Empire with the exposed wood timber frame characteristic of American domestic architecture; for the more academic Dorshreimer house that frame is realized in stone, infilled with brick, and embellished with French Néo-Grec decorative patterns. Richardson's projects for a Civil War Memorial for Worcester, Massachusetts, and Buffalo, New York (1868; 1874), followed the iconographical form of the Arch of Triumph in Paris. For early commercial work for New York and Springfield, Massachusetts, the architect relied upon inspiration found in French publications in his library. The facades of the Western Railroad Offices at Springfield (1867–69), for example, descend from the Italian Renaissance by way of Paul Letarouilly's *Edifices de Rome moderne* or Auguste Grandjean's *Architecture toscane,* both of which he owned. The resulting design was correct, and dry.

Richardson's Worcester High School (1869–71) has been called the nadir of his formative years; it was, in fact, a summation (fig. 18). A building formed without regard to its hillside site, high, gaunt, and awkward, it consisted of a main four-story block with corner pavilions and an underfed central tower and spire. The external walls were a hard red brick laid up with minimal black joints, tattooed with patterns of black pitch, and encrusted around the windows and main entrance with geometrical ornament of the most primitive description. Here the process of design by accumulation produced a jarring and irresolute conformation; here high roofs and pavilions argued with gawky spire; here the bristling freedom of the English picturesque was bridled by the constraint of French classical balance and axial control. This was the work of a neophyte architect of two minds, or rather, of two conflicting available modes of building, and its demolition created more of a historical than a cultural void. Richardson must have sensed his dilemma, for he quickly moved away from such unsatisfactory and unaccomplished melding.

By the time he designed the high school, in the fall of 1869, H. H. had been in practice for three years, had produced at least twenty-five buildings and projects, and had demonstrated his ability to handle the prevailing modes of architectural fashion. He had not, however, distinguished himself from the horde of contemporary practitioners except by the low quality of his achievement. Compared to works by rivals such as George B. Post, Henry Van Brunt, or Richard Morris Hunt during these years, Richardson's early buildings look decidedly second-rate. It is clear to us, and perhaps it eventually dawned upon him, that his abilities were not challenged by designing Gothic churches or mansarded houses. And in the building he designed next after the high school, he broke out of that mold.

The years 1869 to 1872 were extremely important ones for Richardson. He swung away from the stylistic ideals of his contemporaries and began to find his own sources within the architecture of the past. The period begins with Brattle Square Church in Boston (1869–73) and ends with its near neighbor, Trinity, but as usual there is no clear sequential development from the one to the other, just as there is no clear bridge between the high school and Brattle Square, which may have been designed at roughly the same time. Brattle Square (see fig. 30, right) was originally conceived as cruciform in plan, hence a forerunner of Trinity, with a campanile located in one reentrant angle. The walls are local stone and are treated with great simplicity. The openings are round-arched, as is the Clarenden Street arcade, and the sculptural embellishment is restricted to

Frédéric Bartholdi's frieze at the top of the tower, a feature that fixed the building within the developing cityscape of the Back Bay. The church's lithic walls and round-arched openings mark it as a departure from Richardson's earlier work, especially his ecclesiastical work, and the tower has always been justly admired, but the building proved a disaster acoustically. The design is historically important, however, as marking a turning point in H. H.'s search for an appropriate architectural language. Here he seems first to have remembered the lithic, round-arched forms derived from the *Rundbogenstil* that had been the objects of his awakening at Harvard College to

18. H. H. Richardson, high school, Worcester, Massachusetts, 1869–71. Demolished. (Courtesy of the Worcester Historical Museum.)

the art of building. Whether derived from Schulze's college chapel, Bryant's commercial work downtown, or the ecclesiastical Romanesque of Richard Upjohn, the new look achieved by Richardson at Brattle Square set him on his path toward an architecture of personal conviction.

Although Brattle Square was followed in 1871 by two richly picturesque designs for churches, one for Columbus, Ohio, the other for Buffalo, the direction suggested by Brattle Square is paralleled in other building types designed during these years. The Hampden County Courthouse in Springfield (1871–74) develops an axial plan

19. H. H. Richardson, Hampden County Courthouse, Springfield, Massachusetts, 1871–74. Altered. (Courtesy of the Springfield Public Library.)

into a controlled silhouette with central tower (fig. 19). The walls of rock-faced, random ashlar are opened by a round-arched entrance arcade and flat-headed, transomed and mullioned windows. The unsuccessful competition design for the Connecticut State Capitol (1871–72) projected a pyramidal pile of masonry above a cruciform plan, a *parti* directly inspired by the architect's French education. The pyramidal silhouette recurs on a domestic scale in the F. W. Andrews house at Newport (1872–73). And in the North Congregational Church in Springfield (1868, 1871–73), the architect applied his round-arched, simplifying decorative vocabulary to an otherwise run-of-the-mill gable and spire exterior. Clearly he was seeking a language of style distinct from that of his first three years and, just as clearly, he had not yet discovered it.

On 1 June 1872 Richardson won the competition to design Trinity Church in Boston's Back Bay, one of the most important ecclesiastical commissions of the time (see figs. 30, 35, 37). The church, dedicated early in 1877, not only marked the architect's emergence, at the age of thirty-three, as one of the foremost designers in the country, it was a turning point in American cultural history as well (see chapter 3). But the stunning beauty and historical significance of Trinity has led to a misunderstanding of its place in Richardson's career. Here indeed begins the Richardsonian Romanesque, a style that was to sweep the country in the next two decades, but the architect's own style, the unqualified Richardsonian, emerges only after the half-decade of work on Trinity. As we shall see, the church on Copley Square formed the corner-, not the capstone, of his achievement. It brought the search of 1869–72 to dramatic resolution, combining the cruciform plan, the pyramidal mass, the stone wall, and the round arch into architecture of the greatest conviction. It also exemplifies Richardson's design process, learned at the Ecole in Paris, and his shift to recognizable Romanesque precedents as the bases of his eclecticism.

Trinity began to rise beneath the hands of its builders, Norcross Brothers of Worcester, just as the Panic of 1873 deepened. Building activity slowed during the next several years, so Richardson had to wait until near the end of the decade to profit from his achievement and his fame associated with the church.

During these years he accomplished little building, but in what he did accomplish he solidified the stylistic beachhead he had established in the Back Bay. In the Hayden Building in Boston (1875–76; see fig. 46), a commission from his father-in-law, and the Cheney Building in Hartford (1875–76), he transferred his new approach to commercial building (see chapter 4). In the continuation of the work on the State House at Albany (1875 and following), which in association with Leopold Eidlitz and Frederick Law Olmsted he took over from the original designer, Thomas Fuller, he applied it to public architecture. The compromises necessary in this collaborative work, and subsequent changes caused by fire, removal, and other vicissitudes, make it now difficult to assess Richardson's full contribution to the State House, except for the recently restored Senate Chamber. This was designed by Richardson in association with his assistant, Stanford White, beginning in 1876. With the interior of Trinity, the Senate Chamber is the architect's major mid-seventies' achievement in spatial design (fig. 20). The two are related in their rich surfaces and colors surrounding essentially serene, static rooms. Richardson and White began with a raw space some sixty by one hundred feet. Since this was more than was needed for the thirty-two officials then occupying the Senate, they pulled in the side walls, creating lobbies below and visitor's galleries above, and leaving a roughly cubical central vessal. At Trinity Richardson was creating with the artist John La Farge a "color church." Here he and his assistant sought what White called a "piece of color," lining the central space with a rainbow of different natural materials brought from around the world: Mexican onyx panels set in Siena marble frames in the middle register of the north and south walls; the same Italian stone for the gallery arches; Scottish granite columns supporting those arches; gilt leather upper walls; brass chandeliers and sconces; red leather and mahogany lower walls and furniture; a ceiling of oak beams overhead; and a flowered carpet underfoot. Here, as at Trinity, Richardson's genius for order begins to make itself felt. He is in complete control of these diverse materials and colors, seeking, as he wrote to Olmsted, "simplicity and quietness," and accomplishing this by using large geometric forms, broad proportions, sympathetic materials, and a basically cubical space. The richness of this room corresponded to other works of the era; the resulting serenity was Richardson's own gift to American architecture.

With the dedication of Trinity early in 1877, Richardson entered the mature phase of his career; he had but nine years to live. In that brief span his accomplishment was remarkable, for not only did he generate a personal style in architectural design, as we shall see, he also generated a number of styles, varying their application as the problem in hand demanded by its site or its use. The most familiar of these is the Romanesque or, more accurately, the Romanesque-Byzantine-Syrian mode, which he continued to use for some impor-

20. H. H. Richardson, Senate Chamber, New York State Capitol, Albany, 1876–78. Restored. (After Van Rensselaer, *Henry Hobson Richardson and His Works*, 1888.)

tant public buildings through the 1880s. These works include the Ames Memorial Building at North Easton, Massachusetts (1879–81), the City Hall at Albany (1880–83), Austin Hall at Harvard (1881–84), the Ames Wholesale Store on Bedford Street in Boston (1882–83), the Allegheny County Courthouse in Pittsburgh (1883–84; see fig. 28), the Chamber of Commerce Building in Cincinnati (1885–88), and so on. Of course, few of Richardson's buildings of this era are free of some historical detail harking back to Romanesque, Byzantine, or other precedents. He worked within an eclectic era. But his most significant works of the late 1870s and the 1880s display such historic references as minor accents, not form-giving principles of design.

Richardson's use of the Romanesque began at Trinity, if not Brattle Square, but little or nothing from his early period prepares us for the breathtaking power and originality of Sever Hall at Harvard, a work designed with Stanford White in 1878 (fig. 21). With the Ames Free Library at North Easton of the previous year (see figs. 24–25), Sever forms the portal to Richardson's maturity, the years in which he gained full command of his resources. Sever was commissioned on a limited budget to be a basic barn of a building housing classrooms reached by a central hall, stair, and double-loaded corridors. What Richardson made of this restricted commission is extraordinary, recalling the old saw that the architect designs best who is limited most, for here he first fully disciplined the picturesque, here he first announced to the world that American culture had not only come of age (that he had accomplished at Trinity), but was capable of generating ideas independent of French, English, or German pressure. The design takes its cues from its site in Harvard Yard and across from Bulfinch's University Hall. Its materials and its balanced form focused upon a central axis reflect the existing Georgian and Federal structures of the old college. Certain forms, too, hark back to the classical past, such as the central pediment facing the Yard and the pedimented frontispiece facing Quincy Street. Within this historical framework, Richardson first created that "quiet and monumental treatment of wall surfaces" which he said formed his chief aim as a mature designer. The red brick block is capped by an orange tile hip roof. Openings are organized into continuous horizontal zones, and these are echoed by the decorative belt courses, the water table, the eave, and the roof ridge. The work is monochromatic, compact, contained. The building is conceived as a whole within which repetitive parts are organized into supporting roles. So, for example, the dormer on the Quincy Street side of the roof is pulled into one long

21. H. H. Richardson, Sever Hall, Harvard University, 1878–80. (After Van Rensselaer, *Henry Hobson Richardson and His Works,* 1888.)

22. William Ware and Henry Van Brunt, Memorial Hall, Harvard University, 1867–78. (Photo by A. H. Folsom; courtesy of the Boston Athenaeum, gift of Mrs. Harrison Schock from the estate of Frank I. Cooper.)

horizontal echoing the reiterative horizontals mounting from ground line to ridge. So, for example, the molded chimneys are broad and squat, barely rising above the ridge. Such tightly disciplined design could have produced a dull, lifeless building, but Sever is vibrantly alive within its restraints. The hip roof flares out over the eaves; half-circular bays body forth from the long facades; molded bricks toss light and shadow patterns around the openings; and carved brick flora and fauna enrich the exterior at strategic points. The subtle yet powerful building was Richardson's manifesto. It is dramatically different from the polychromatic, picturesque piles of contemporaries such as William Ware and Henry Van Brunt, whose Ruskin-inspired, High Victorian Gothic Memorial Hall at Harvard (1865–78) stands a stone's throw from Sever in space but miles from it in effect (fig. 22). In contrast to Memorial Hall and like designs, Sever was fresh and new, a work of architecture to which might be applied Larzer Ziff's characterization of Emerson as an "escape from history . . . a true American beginning."

The brick used at Sever was called for by the predominantly brick architecture of old Harvard, but it was not to be the characteristic material of Richardson's maturity. For the majority of his buildings the architect chose rock-faced granite ashlar enriched with red East Longmeadow sandstone in the late 1870s and early 1880s (see fig. 25) and monochromatic layered ashlar in his last works (see fig. 29). The shift from random to layered stonework is indicative of his concern to create increasingly unified buildings in contrast to the additive compositions of his peers. The detailing is in the main superb, because Richardson from Trinity Church on had a personal builder as talented in his field as the architect was in his. Orlando Whitney Norcross, whose firm supplied not only the stonemasons but also the stone itself, habitually collaborated with the architect from early on in a design, and the influence of his standard of excellence can be felt in every detail of a Richardson building erected under his care. One key to Richardson's success is to be found in his ability to organize into an effective team a variety of highly talented individuals such as Norcross, Stanford White, Charles McKim, F. L. Olmsted, John La Farge, Augustus Saint-Gaudens, and many others. The mature Richardson building was a synthesis no less of talent and materials than of recurrent design motifs.

Even before the synthesis in brick at Sever, Richardson had applied his discipline to stone at the Ames Library of 1877, the second in the series of suburban libraries he was to design in the last years of his life. In the first, the Winn Memorial at Woburn, Massachusetts

23. H. H. Richardson, Winn Memorial Library, Woburn, Massachusetts, 1876–79. (Photo by Jean Baer O'Gorman.)

(1876–79), he analyzed the building program into a diagrammatic plan combining natural history museum, picture gallery, reading room, and book alcoves, and expressed that analysis through the multiplex polychromatic forms of its exterior to produce a richly dramatic building distinguishable from contemporary picturesque work only by its heavy Romanesque details (fig. 23). It is a model of picturesque eclecticism (see chapter 3). At the Ames Library (fig. 24), the absence of museum and picture gallery allows for a simpler analysis followed by an integration of parts to produce a unified design. The whole is drawn into a more compact silhouette and the details are reduced in number and simplified in form. A horizontal organizing principle is applied to the elevations to impose order. This is especially evident in the alcove wing (fig. 25), where the mass is reduced to three superimposed horizontal zones—a base of random ashlar masonry set in red mortar and articulated only by the water table, which rises to the continuous sill beneath a friezelike zone punctuated by repetitive window voids. The frieze terminates at the eave, above which is the simple hip roof capped by an emphatic horizontal

24. H. H. Richardson, Ames Memorial Library, North Easton, Massachusetts, 1877–78. (Photo by the author).

25. Ames Library, detail of exterior. (After Van Rensselaer, *Henry Hobson Richardson and His Works,* 1888.)

ridge. The disciplining process imposed at the Ames Library carried on to its conclusion at the Crane Library at Quincy, Massachusetts (1880–82; see fig. 70). Here the silhouette is contained by upright walls and horizontal ridge, as the front gable and the squat stair tower are compacted within the outline. The detail remains borrowed from the past, but the effect of the building scarcely depends on the fact (see chapter 6).

The evolution of design witnessed by the succession of libraries beginning with the Winn Memorial and ending with the Crane is a concentrated reflection of the direction of Richardson's career in general. He began as an eclectic composer but he quickly began to apply the governing principles of composition learned at the Ecole, and the simplifying lithic forms of the Romanesque and *Rundbogenstil,* eventually as a mature designer creating the large, simple, massive works of his last years. To discipline the picturesque was his aim and his achievement.

"I'll plan anything a man wants," the architect said to one of his late clients, J. J. Glessner, "from a cathedral to a chicken coop." And indeed, with the revival of building after the hiatus of the mid-1870s, Richardson's practice developed into a well-rounded one. Domestic design formed a large part of his office work, but there were also public buildings, railroad stations (see chapter 6), ecclesiastical work, commercial buildings (see chapter 4), and more libraries. In the early eighties, too, his practice began to take on national dimensions, as it spread first to Washington then westward to Pittsburgh, Cincinnati, Detroit, Chicago, and, finally, St. Louis (not to mention one monument in Wyoming; see chapter 5). To the Brahmin clientele of his early career he added the self-made capitalists of the emerging Middle West, men such as Marshall Field and J. J. Glessner. The range of the architect's mature design services can be seen by looking first at relatively modest domestic works, such as the Stoughton house at Cambridge (1882–83) and the J. J. Glessner house in Chicago (1885–87) and then at the largest of his commissions and his crowning achievement, at least in his own mind, the Allegheny County Buildings at Pittsburgh.

The Stoughton house (fig. 26) is a wooden variation of the disciplined forms of Sever Hall or the Crane Library. It is one of the outstanding examples of what Vincent Scully long ago labeled the "shingle style," the American version of the English Shavian or Queen Anne mode. The L-shaped plan is characteristic of the shingle style in general, centered upon a living hall with fireplace and stair. The exterior is all of a piece, the various units rendered as simple geometric forms without ornament, the whole pulled together by the shingled membranes surrounding the inner volumes. Surfaces flow together; windows are broken into transoms and mullions to carry the scale of the shingle across the void of the opening; the horizontal prevails, from the flared ground line to the shingled ridge. Although Richardson was not solely responsible for the shingle style, in the Stoughton house, as in the John Bryant house at Cohasset, Massachusetts (1880–81), and especially in the demolished H. S. Potter house in St. Louis (1886–87), he created some of its most memorable images.

The Glessner house (fig. 27) is to stone what the Stoughton is to shingles. It too is L-shaped in plan, with the hall tucked into the angle and embellished with fireplace and stair. This, the domestic equivalent to the architect's commercial achievement in the Marshall Field Wholesale Store in the same city (see chapter 4), appears as a granite fortress from the corner of Prairie and Eighteenth streets. Despite the change in material, the qualities of wholeness and repose

26. H. H. Richardson, Stoughton house, Cambridge, Massachusetts, 1882–83. (Courtesy of the Boston Athenaeum, gift of Mrs. Harrison Schock from the estate of Frank I. Cooper.)

27. H. H. Richardson, J. J. Glessner house, Chicago, 1885–87. (Photo by George Glessner, ca. 1887; courtesy of the Chicago Architecture Foundation.)

we find at the Stoughton house are reiterated here. The horizontal recurs repeatedly, since the stonework is monochromatic layered ashlar set in red mortar, and ornament is minimal. The design depends, as do all of Richardson's finest mature works, upon the coordination of the basic elements of architecture: form, material, scale, relationship of solid to void, and so on. Here the "quiet and monumental" is fully realized; here is a Richardsonian building without historical qualification.

The 1885 poll of architects that selected five of Richardson's works as among the ten best in the United States must have gratified the ailing architect, and helped to confirm his sense of accomplishment. But the buildings honored included, besides Trinity, the Albany City Hall, Sever, the State House at Albany, and the Memorial Hall at North Easton, suggesting with that assortment that his peers were not entirely clear about his achievement. And the architect knew he had not yet reached the pinnacle of his powers. It was probably this listing that prompted him to utter the oft-quoted statement that "if they honor me for the pigmy things I have already done, what will they say when they see Pittsburgh finished?" It was Richardson's one wish (which he was not granted) to live long enough to see the Allegheny County Courthouse and Jail completed. He thought of the complex as the capstone of his career. Whereas we might now see the railroad stations, the Ames Gate Lodge, and the Marshall Field Wholesale Store as more historically important, and perhaps even intrinsically better works, the public buildings at Pittsburgh are indeed completely realized works of the architect's maturity, and in size, location, and chronology hold a special place with regard to the "pigmy things" he created elsewhere.

28. H. H. Richardson, Allegheny County Courthouse, Pittsburgh, 1883–88. (After Van Rensselaer, *Henry Hobson Richardson and His Works,* 1888.)

The complex consists of two elements, the courthouse and the jail, and each exemplifies a different aspect of the architect's maturity. The courthouse (fig. 28) is a place of public access and collective will demanding dramatic profile and ornamental detail. These symbolic requirements, however, are wedded to the practical considerations of a building intended for large public gatherings requiring ease of access, clarity of circulation, and optimum natural lighting and ventilation. The plan is an axial arrangement of courtrooms off a single-loaded corridor surrounding a central courtyard. The section through the building was so designed that each of the main courtrooms was lighted from two sides. An advanced heating and ventilating system based on that used in the Houses of Parliament in London, an arrangement the architect had studied during his trip abroad in 1882, was designed to take in air through circular nostrils at the top of the main tower, treat it in the basement, distribute it throughout the building, and expel it at the tops of the secondary towers at the rear of the courtyard. So the building's spiky silhouette was born of mechanical need rather than stylistic preference, although it did have its expressive use (before the erection of surrounding commercial high-risers) of identifying this as an important public building within the urban pattern. Within and without, the building is animated by Romanesque columns, arches, and minimal ornament, although, as usual in even the most decorative of Richardson's late works, in the overall effect of the courthouse such historical references have a secondary role. It is the elemental architectural relationships that shine forth here: the superb monochromatic stonework of the exterior walls, its alternating wide and narrow layered ashlar set in red mortar contrasting with the simpler treatment of the courtyard; the play of solid and void; the richly articulated forms; the dramatic arched spaces of the entry and stairhall; and the originally exposed metallic framing of the courtrooms (a feature rare in the architect's work). These combined to make of the Pittsburgh courthouse one of the most distinguished public buildings in America.

The elemental architectural relationships we can discern through the ornamental detail of the courthouse become the overriding characteristics of the jail (fig. 29). The richness of carved ornament appropriate for the exterior and interior of the public structure would have been inappropriate for the punitive program of this limited-access building. The plan of the cell block is a traditional, radial one, with wings of stacked cubicles branching outward from a multi-tiered, central control point. This is encased within a high stone wall, a solid mass of rock-faced layered ashlar set in red mortar,

29. H. H. Richardson, Allegheny County Jail, Pittsburgh, 1883–88. (Photo by Wayne Andrews.)

relieved only by the water table running along at mid-height, which forms one of the most monumental and memorable examples of the stonemason's art in America. This austere exterior is relieved only sparingly by square-cut windows and round-arched openings. One of the latter is a monumental archway that might be the single most characteristic example of Richardson's mature style. This is a half-circle that springs from the ground. The void is created by a series of rock-faced voussoirs some eight feet long, following examples Richardson had seen in Spain, their effect undiluted by archivolts or other ornamental interruptions. This is elemental architecture; this is the "quiet and monumental" design of which the architect spoke. This is a building which relies for its effect upon the basic materials and geometry of construction. If the courthouse may fairly be called Richardsonian Romanesque (in its finest manifestation), the jail may just as fairly be called, simply, Richardsonian. We need not wonder that the architect longed for life sufficient to witness the realization of his crowning achievement in public architecture.

In a brief twenty years Richardson had developed from a neophyte struggling to master contemporary styles to a master of his own style. His juggling of English and French sources in his early works proved alien to his need to create a monumental architecture appropriate to post–Civil War America. Gradually he shifted his dependence from contemporary modes to a more distant historical source of inspiration, seeking in the great stone buildings of Romanesque France and Spain the elemental basis upon which he might build. His use of that source material varied from close emulation to free adaptation to surpassing reinterpretation. His aim was not merely to shift the historical focus within his eclectic era, but to bring order to architectural design, to discipline the picturesque, to create massive but quiet and simple buildings expressive of their basic programmatic needs. His undergraduate observations in Cambridge and Boston of the new architecture within the local granite tradition first introduced him to such building. His training at the Ecole des Beaux-Arts in Paris furthered this direction through ordered planning and controlled composition. And his subsequent study in books and on the ground of the primitive medieval forms of the Auvergne and elsewhere gave him a reinvigorated lithic vocabulary with which to begin realizing his mature aims. But Richardson also had to turn to other sources, not all of them strictly architectural, to fulfill completely the central aspect of his architectural program. For, it would seem, he sought not to build Romanesque buildings in the New World, but to create evolved architectural forms which by association would express the pluralistic American society of the post–Civil War years.

3 • *Eclecticism*

The selection of . . . elements from various . . . sources . . . for the purpose of combining them into a satisfying . . . style.

Webster's Third New International Dictionary

Trinity Church on Copley Square in Boston is usually characterized as Richardson's finest work (fig. 30; see also figs. 35, 37). It is indeed a powerful presence; it is indeed among this country's most satisfying ecclesiastical designs, but it is also a creation of awakening convictions, not of mature achievement. It is the cornerstone, not the capstone, of the architect's career. At the same time, with its dedication in the year following the national centennial in 1876, Trinity represented American culture's coming of age.

The creation of Trinity brought together a group of relatively young men who were to be important in the cultural awakening of the United States after the Civil War. The Reverend Phillips Brooks, a gifted orator, was rector of Trinity and later the Episcopal bishop of Massachusetts. Charles F. McKim and Stanford White, two of the leading architects of the next generation, began their careers at Trinity as Richardson's chief assistants. The builder, O. W. Norcross of Norcross Brothers of Worcester, was to become a major figure in the development of general contracting in this country. The painter and decorator John La Farge and the

30. (*Left*) Alfred H. Schroff, *New Old South, Trinity, and Brattle Square Churches,* Back Bay, Boston, ca. 1878. H. H. Richardson's Trinity Church (1872–77) forms the centerpiece of this painting after a photograph of 1877. (From the collection of the Shawmut Bank of Boston, N.A.)

sculptor Augustus Saint-Gaudens were foremost in the development of American arts in the last quarter of the nineteenth century. And Henry Adams made the decoration of Trinity, although he changed its name to St. John's and its location to New York, the setting for his novel *Esther* (1884). The church was the first important work of America's first architect of major international significance, and it contains the first large-scale decorative program conceived and executed by native American (albeit, like Richardson, European-trained) artists. The interior of the church is one of the most serene architectural spaces in the world. The building stands with the contemporary novels of Mark Twain (*Tom Sawyer,* 1876) and the contemporary paintings of Thomas Eakins (*The Gross Clinic,* 1875) and Winslow Homer (*Breezing Up!,* 1876) at the rising summit of nineteenth-century American cultural achievement.

Trinity congregation voted late in 1870 to move from the old center of Boston into the heart of the new fashionable residential district known, because it was created by filling in the tidal flats west of the Common, as the Back Bay. A building committee headed by

31. Letter from the building committee of Trinity Church, Boston, with autograph sketches by H. H. Richardson, 1872. (Courtesy of the Department of Printing and Graphic Arts, Houghton Library, Harvard University.)

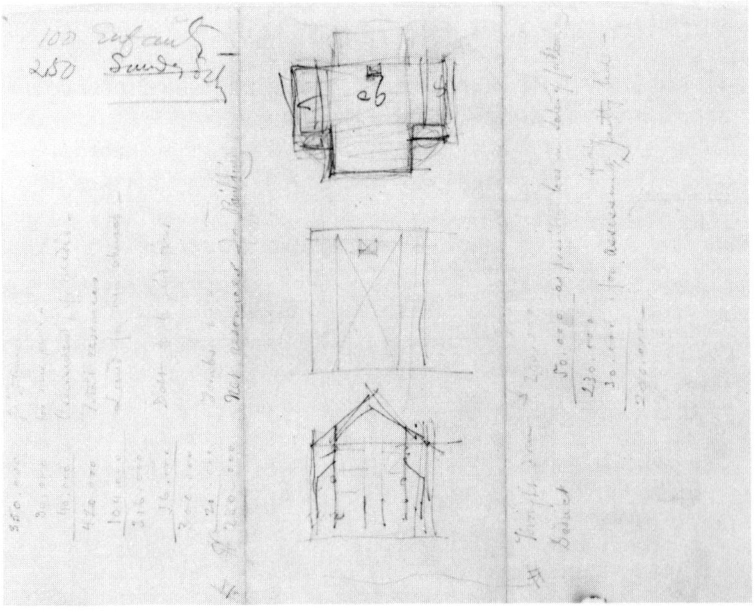

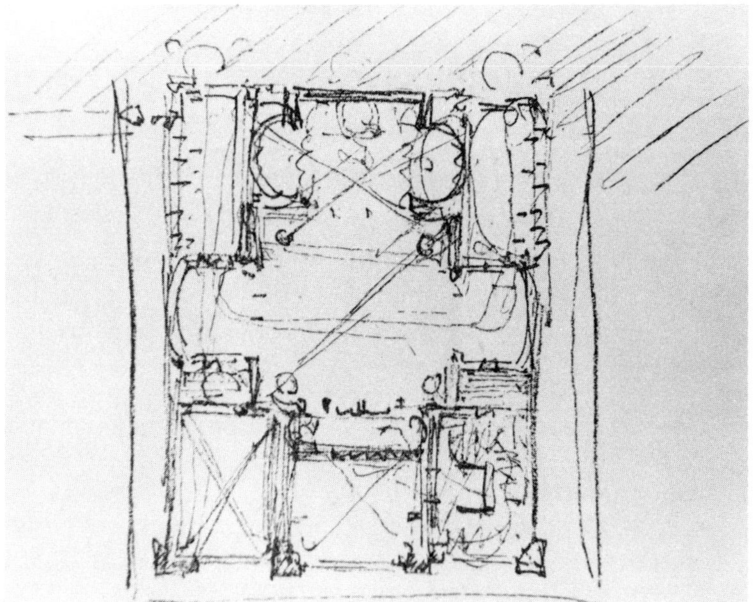

32. H. H. Richardson, sketch plan for a casino project, 1863. (After Van Rensselaer, *Henry Hobson Richardson and His Works,* 1888.)

Robert Treat Paine invited Richardson and six other Boston and New York architects of more mature reputation to compete for the commission to design a new church. In June 1872 Richardson (nominally in association with Charles Gambrill) was named the architect; after several design modifications during construction, the congregation dedicated its new sanctuary in February 1877. It was Richardson's first work of more than local significance, and he made the most of his opportunity.

When H. H. received the letter of the building committee requesting him to participate in the design competition, he turned it over and rapidly sketched alternate schemes, one for a basilical church with clerestory, the other, the source of the final building, a Greek cross (fig. 31). In his initial reaction to the building program described in the letter, the architect was proceeding according to the process of design he had learned at the Ecole in Paris. There, as we know from his 1863 project for a casino (fig. 32), he was taught to begin with a rapid notation, or *esquisse,* resolving the program into its simplest conformation. With this thumbnail sketch, or better, ideogram, for a guide, he could proceed to develop the plan in detail.

33. H. H. Richardson, preliminary sketch for the Cathedral of All Saints, Albany, 1882. (Courtesy of the Department of Printing and Graphic Arts, Houghton Library, Harvard University.)

The three-dimensional mass was studied in the same way, as witnessed by Richardson's quick graphic for the elevation of All Saint's, Albany (1882; fig. 33). This method focused the designer's attention upon the *parti,* or central design idea, and provided a measure of control for all subsequent stages in the development of the final drawings and hence of the resulting building. Here began Richardson's grasp of the building as a whole to which all details could be subordinated. For many of his later works the only drawings from his hand we possess are such ideograms, his contribution to the graphic process being concentrated in what Van Rensselaer called the "initial impulse." Developmental drawings were produced by assistants under his "constant criticism." The degree of control he achieved in his design of Trinity Church is directly traceable to the original ideograms he sketched on the back of the invitation to compete. As Richardson matured, this control, this discipline, came more and more to govern his work.

Trinity's restrained pyramidal silhouette was in part the result of this initial graphic impulse, this controlling ideogram, but it also stemmed from the conditions of the site and from the architect's selection of stylistic sources. The Back Bay plot was a trapezoid of fill bounded on all sides by city streets; the area to the west was eventually to develop into Copley Square. Four thousand five hundred wooden piles were driven into the tidal ooze and the building erected upon that floating "raft." The shape and underpinnings of the site ultimately dictated the centralized plan and squat tower of the final design, and hence the low pyramidal outline of the exterior, for the engineers thought the high profile of the original drawings would require a tower too heavy for the existing conditions.

As did his contemporaries, Richardson selected European historical sources for his design, but his use of them was highly personal. Trinity, in his own words, was "a free rendering of the French Romanesque," with the emphasis on freedom. The architect was more interested in "quiet and monumental" architecture, more interested in stability and repose, than in the accuracy of borrowed design. From the cruciform plan the exterior walls of Dedham granite

34. Salamanca, Old Cathedral, lantern. (After G. E. Street, *Some Account of Gothic Architecture in Spain*, 1865.)

ashlar set in red mortar and trimmed with light red East Longmeadow sandstone rise to create four relatively short arms rotating from a central mass. The architect chose as model for this central feature the cupola of the Romanesque cathedral of Salamanca in Spain (fig. 34) but transformed it into the controlling motif of his exterior composition. Whereas the architects of his day usually employed in church design an asymmetrical tower to create a dynamic silhouette, as did Cummings and Sears at contemporary New Old South Church across Copley Square (see fig. 30, left), Richardson sought to discipline the effect of his mass. "The struggle for precedence which often takes place between a Church and its spire," he wrote in his 1877 description of his building, "was disposed of, by at once and completely subordinating nave, transepts, and apse, and grouping them about the tower as central mass" (see fig. 37). The result was the pyramidal external form which was long the visual anchor for Copley Square.

Richardson left the exterior of his church unfinished. It was not until nearly a decade after his death that the elaborate western turrets and the ornate porch were added from designs of his successors, Shepley, Rutan, and Coolidge. Based closely on the porch of the Romanesque church of St. Trôphime at Arles in the south of France, the new entrance is an act of high-quality historicism that points up the freedom with which Richardson himself employed the Romanesque in the rest of the building.

The interior of Trinity was shaped for the renowned preaching voice of Phillips Brooks (fig. 35). The wide arms of the plan open through broad round arches into the vast auditorium beneath the tower to carry into the interior the sense of serenity and repose that marks the exterior of the building. Richardson sought what he called the "rich effect of color in the interior," a characteristic he must have admired in the 1864 Prix de Rome project for a Romanesque church with polychromatic interior designed by his friend, Julien Guadet. At Trinity Richardson achieved his desire in collaboration with the finest native decorative talent available. The only earlier extensive decorative program in the country was to be found in the Capitol at Washington, but that was largely the work of imported artists. John La Farge and his American assistants decorated Trinity with monumental biblical figures set against a dark red field. La Farge and others, including eventually English and French makers, enriched the window openings with colored glass, in the modern development of which La Farge was rivaled only by his compatriot, Louis Comfort Tiffany. La Farge's triple lancet window above the western entrance,

35. Trinity Church, interior. (Photo by Richard Cheek.)

36. Furness and Hewitt, Pennsylvania Academy of the Fine Arts, Philadelphia, facade, 1871–76. (Courtesy of the Pennsylvania Academy of the Fine Arts Archives.)

with vertical fields of sparkling aqua glass flanking a full-length figure of Christ, are breathtaking when afternoon sunlight penetrates the richly coloristic pattern. The result of light filtering through colored glass and reflecting from colored walls is to make the space of this interior seem palpable. Shadow and color scatter the emptiness, suffusing the interior, filling the void. The *Boston Evening Transcript* noted at the dedication "a solidity and grandeur of [interior] effect not to be described, but to be seen and felt." The evasive quality of the room cannot be better suggested.

From the moment of its dedication Trinity was recognized by populace and professionals alike as a work distinct from the run-of-the-mill ecclesiastical architecture of the day. It was indeed different, in quality, and in the architect's use and control of historical raw materials, but it was similar in his adherence to a fundamental characteristic of contemporary design to which the term "eclecticism"—as opposed to "historicism"—has been applied. Eclecticism was as endemic in American architecture after the Civil War as historicism had been in the first half of the century. "Historicism" here means the use of past styles in which the integrity of the source is respected, or nearly so, in the recreated design. The pure temple form of the Greek

Revival of the 1820s, although often in public buildings modified by the Roman vault and in domestic work framed with traditional timbers or balloon sticks, was intended to recall the Hellenic original. Its use, following the principle of associationism, linked the political ideals of the fledgling democracy (or republic) with their ancient antecedents. So, too, the English Perpendicular Gothic Revival church of the 1840s, however naively it aped its medieval ancestors, was meant to draw its symbolism from the Anglo-Christian past. Although in practice anything was possible, even a Greco-Gothic meeting house—its white wooden shape temple-like, its windows pointed—in principle by the 1840s at least, mingling of the physical manifestations of differing cultures or periods was abhorred, and misapplication, as in the use of the pagan temple for a Christian church, condemned.

After the war such purity of association seemed too simple, and architecture in America became eclectic. Frank Furness's Pennsylvania Academy of the Fine Arts on Broad Street in Philadelphia (1871–76), for example, combines a neoclassical *parti,* a French Second Empire pavilion, North Italian Gothic openings filtered through Ruskin's works, and details inspired by both English and French sources, including the publications of Viollet-le-Duc (fig. 36). Any historical recall in this potpourri aims toward Babel! Design by accumulation became the norm in the 1870s; progressive thought justified it. As the architect Henry Van Brunt put it in the introduction to his translation of Viollet-le-Duc's *Discourses* (1875): "art . . . must . . . proceed by derivation and development; and where architectural monuments and traditions have accumulated to the vast extent they have in modern times, the question is not whether we [Americans] shall use them at all, but how shall we choose among them, and to what extent shall such choice be allowed to influence our modern practice."

The eclectic building, a veritable anthology of parts selected and combined from the whole of building history east and west, became the standard in the years after 1860. It usually took the form of polychromatic details piled into an irregular, or "picturesque," silhouette, a richly varied concoction of medieval and/or classical (and, at times, oriental) pieces. Despite the wholesale destruction of buildings of this era that occurred in the years immediately following World War II, nearly every city, town, village, or hamlet in the country, if it existed before the 1870s, to this day sports such an example of "Victorian excess."

Richardson's approach to the design of Trinity was as eclectic as that for any other building of the time. Both his winning competitive design of 1872 and the modified, erected church of 1877 were put together according to an accumulative system of composition. As Ann Adams has observed, "Richardsonian Romanesque was [here] . . . a combination of principles learned in France with the picturesque and massive forms of contemporary English work." Trinity's plan was born of the *esquisse* project of the Ecole, and developed by the application of rational geometry—the square of the crossing determining other relationships—also derived from the architect's training in Paris. The three-dimensional massing followed the lead of

37. Trinity Church, east end. The silhouette stems from French Romanesque; the tower, from Spain. (After *Monographs of American Architecture* 5, 1888.)

the Romanesque churches of the Auvergne, in which, as Richardson wrote in 1877, "the tower became, as it were, the church, and the composition took the outline of a pyramid" (figs. 37–38). But the tower in Richardson's competitive design is closer to English ecclesiastical precedents in its high profile, and to Dutch and Flemish town-hall towers in its details, than to those of his French models, and the tower finally erected was, as we have seen, adapted from that of the old cathedral of Salamanca. Since the architect first visited Spain in the summer of 1882, he must have known his source from an intermediate publication, perhaps a photograph sent by a traveling

38. Brioud, east end, twelfth century. The octagonal tower is a mid-nineteenth-century reconstruction. (Photo by Jean Baer O'Gorman.)

39. H. H. Richardson, competition drawing of the facade of All Saints, Albany, 1882. (After Van Rensselaer, *Henry Hobson Richardson and His Works*, 1888.)

friend, perhaps a plate in G. E. Street's *Gothic Architecture in Spain* (1865), a copy of which he owned (see fig. 34). In this design process, in which the architect imitates the proverbial magpie, Richardson was thoroughly a man of his eclectic era.

But Trinity also heralded the presence of a designer distinct from his peers. What set it apart was the architect's selection of source materials from the Romanesque, a historical style distinct in itself from either the classical or Gothic sources favored by his contemporaries, and the way he combined his parts. As he said of the Romanesque in general, it differed from the classical "in that, while it studied elegance, it was also constructional," and it differed from the Gothic "in that, although constructional, it would sacrifice something of mechanical dexterity for the sake of grandeur and repose." A constructional (and lithic) style of grandeur and repose: this was what Richardson sought in the Romanesque. He was attracted by its overall effect, not its accumulating detail.

At Trinity, according to Van Rensselaer, Richardson used the Romanesque "which he had just begun to study" as the basis of his design. Ten years later, after his journey of 1882, "he was fresh from the study of ancient Romanesque art [in France and Spain] and more than ever convinced of its peculiar fitness for modern adaptation." The latter remark occurs in connection with her discussion of a second ecclesiastical competition in which Richardson submitted a project derived from the Romanesque, that for All Saint's Cathedral in Albany (1882; fig. 39). He did not win, and, indeed, must never have thought he could, since he ignored the stipulation that the design be "Gothic in style." His stubborn adherence to his chosen path suggests the depth of his conviction that the Romanesque held the best possibilities for naturalization in nineteenth-century America. But the design shown in his competition drawings, which he did hope he might modify, lacks the vitality achieved at Trinity merely because of the latter's tentative nature.

At Trinity Richardson inaugurated the "Richardsonian Romanesque," a style which quickly swept the country. Its popularity was affirmed by the architects' poll of 1885, and reaffirmed by every imitation of Trinity erected in the 1880s and 1890s from east coast to west. The style, in fact, was more commonly employed by followers than by its innovator, followers who often failed to notice that the essence of Richardson's achievement did not depend simply upon his choice of historical materials but upon the principles of composition the architect learned at the Ecole des Beaux-Arts reinforced by his study of those materials. Thus, many a Richardsonian Romanesque building is in reality a picturesque eclectic pile employing Romanesque rather than Victorian Gothic or other forms. Arthur Vinal's Water Department Building in the Boston suburb of Chestnut Hill (1887) is a prime example of what might better be labeled "Picturesque Romanesque" (fig. 40). The use of the nominal adjective associating the style with Richardson does his memory an injustice.

Richardson did from time to time avail himself of decidedly Romanesque forms in buildings erected after Trinity. These include the Winn Memorial Library (see fig. 23), Austin Hall at Harvard, and the late Cincinnati Chamber of Commerce Building, none of which would now be included in a list of his most satisfying works. The specific details of the Romanesque held little meaning for him. At Trinity he employed the Auvergnac model for certain reasons of site

40. Arthur Vinal, pumping station, Chestnut Hill, Massachusetts, 1887. (Photo by the author.)

and effect, but he was not a scholar determined upon the peculiarities of historic detail. As he wrote in his description of the unfinished sculpture of Trinity, "the distinguishing characteristics of a style are independent of details; especially is this the case in the Romanesque, which in its treatment of masses, affords an inexhaustible source of study quite independent of its merits as a school of sculpture." Richardson sought in the style its massive effect, its grandeur and repose, and these he attempted to emulate at Trinity despite the eclecticism of his approach.

It is this attitude which, ultimately, distinguishes Richardson from contemporary designers. For them composition was the accumulation of detail, of the piling of feature upon feature. For him, even at Trinity, in this most eclectic, and in truth, inchoate work, detail was fundamentally subordinated to a unifying principle of composition which sought the large effect of simple lithic forms piled into a pyramidal mass shaping a vast, coherent auditorium. If Trinity saw the birth of the Richardsonian Romanesque, it also saw the first imposition of discipline upon the picturesque eclecticism of the period. Trinity does not realize the full potential of that discipline. It is tentative as an expression of Richardson's personal contribution to American architecture. It is a promising but not a realized statement.

So to position it in relation to Richardson's career and the development of late nineteenth-century American architecture, however, is not to deny it its inherent power as an ecclesiastical design. We can without hesitation agree with those fellow Boston architects who, on a plaque installed in the courtyard of the church in 1913, labeled Trinity "his noblest work," and we can unblushingly extend that reference to say that it is among America's noblest buildings. To single it out, however, as Richardson's masterpiece, to call it his most characteristic design, is to misunderstand the architect's multifaceted contribution to the shaping of American architecture. Trinity first brought Richardson to world renown, and it was his first attempt to create a personal architecture that would transfer the history of monumental lithic design from the Old World to the New, but it was only in works such as the Marshall Field Wholesale Store in Chicago (see fig. 41), the Ames gate lodge in North Easton, Massachusetts (see fig. 56), and in several railroad depots and small-town libraries (see figs. 65, 70) that Richardson fully realized his aim. It is to these products of city, suburb, country, and their connectors that we must now turn.

4 • *Urbanism*

A monument to trade, to the organized commercial spirit, to the power and progress of the age.

Louis H. Sullivan

In 1868, about the time he first met Richardson, Frederick Law Olmsted issued a report on his own work at Riverside, Illinois, in which he clearly recognized the major social forces acting to produce the post–Civil War American environment with its densely packed commercial cores, its outlying domestic retreats, and its need for workable connectors between the two. In his lecture on public parks two years later at Boston's Lowell Institute, the landscape architect demanded that the special needs of these distinct zones be met by a variety of forms. It is a basic assumption of this study that his new friend Richardson was to make this environmental vision the framework of his architectural program.

The inclusive character of H. H.'s practice was recognized by Van Rensselaer when she wrote that "town and rural work; municipal buildings, libraries and churches; railroad stations and dwellings; wholesale warehouses and retail stores; bridges, monuments, fountains, armories, succeeded each other beneath his busy hand." Richardson may never have had the opportunity to design a grain elevator or the interior of a river steamboat, as he said he wished to do, but he did meet with success with the various other design challenges of his day. His practice was comprehensive, unlike those of successors such as Louis Sullivan or Frank Lloyd Wright, each of whom was primarily associated with one building type. For each of Olmsted's social zones the mature Richardson gradually evolved a special architectural image. For important urban public works he resorted, from time to time, to his Romanesque or, better, to his eclectic Romanesque-Byzantine-Syrian vocabulary developed after Trinity. For suburban or rural domestic work he used either the shingle style for wooden buildings or, as it will be called in the proper place (see chapter 5), the geological image when stone was the primary material. For the commuter lines leading into the commercial core he developed the hip-sheltered railroad depot (see chapter 6). And for the urban center itself he gave us the urbane dwelling (such as the Glessner house) and the blockbuster commercial building. Richardson shaped American architecture by looking for inspiration first to the great stone buildings of the Romanesque past, then to New England and eventually to North American continental sources, and then adapting these ideas to the diverse conditions of use and site presented by the individual building program. We never learn this from the words of the architect, who wrote very little of theoretical value, but we do have the testimony of contemporaries, which suggests that he sought to create architecture for the New World that would build upon that of the Old without merely aping it. Van Rensselaer, for example, tells us he often remarked that "it would not cost me a bit of trouble to build French buildings . . . , but that is not what I want to do." And his collaborator, the artist John La Farge, once remarked that Richardson "was obliged . . . to throw overboard in dealing with new problems all his educational recipes learned in other countries." But more cogently, we have the witness of Richardson's mature works. From these we may deduce that the architect intended his buildings as an American expression. As American society began to break into urban and suburban zones, he sought to articulate a variety of appropriate architectural responses. In this chapter we follow him into the commercial core.

By the 1880s the wealth of the United States, once derived from and expressed by control of vast expanses of land or sea, had begun to concentrate in and take expression from the physical density of the burgeoning commercial centers. What had been before mid-century an agrarian people was to become by 1900 a largely urban one. This process, wrote Arthur Schlesinger in *The Rise of the City,* in the 1880s "for the first time became a controlling factor in national life." In the city, he continued, "were focused all the new economic forces: the vast accumulations of capital, the business and financial institutions, the spreading railway yards, the gaunt smoky mills, the white-collar middle classes, the motley wage-earning population."

Perhaps nowhere was this facet of American national development more dramatically manifest than in the couple of square miles on the western shore of Lake Michigan known today as Chicago's Loop, its central business gridiron. By the mid-1860s Chicago had become the hub of an extensive rail network, the supplier of goods for the expanding western territories. By the mid-1880s the city was a concentration of three-quarters of a million people serving an area of nearly half a million square miles with a dispersed population of about eleven million. It had survived a holocaust (1871) and rebuilt itself into the most powerful commercial center of mid-America. It radiated wealth and energy; it was, in Carl Sandburg's well-worn 1916 verse, "Tool Maker / Stacker of Wheat / Player with Railroads / . . . Stormy, husky, brawling / City of the Big Shoulders." And so it struck the observant traveler in the 1880s. In *Studies in the South and West* (1889), Charles Dudley Warner wrote that "it is the business portion [of Chicago] . . . that is the miracle of the time, the solid creation of energy and capital since the fire—the square mile containing the Post Office and City Hall, the giant hotels, the opera-houses and theatres, the Board of Trade building, the many-storied offices, the great shops, the club houses, the vast retail and wholesale warehouses. This area has the advantage of some other great business centres in having broad streets at right angles, but with all this openness for movement, the throng of passengers and traffic, the intersecting street and cable railways, the loads of freight and the crush of carriages, the life and hurry and excitement are sufficient to satisfy the most eager lover of metropolitan pandemonium."

The perfect concentration of big-shouldered economic energy, the focus of the expansive trade network, was the wholesale district along the Chicago River on the north and west sides of the center, and within that district one building stood out among the others. "The wholesale warehouse of Marshall Field, the work of that truly original American architect, Richardson, which in massiveness, simplicity of lines, and admirable blending of artistic beauty with adaptability to its purpose," seemed to Warner "unrivalled in this country." It was more than that to another sharp observer of contemporary building and society. For Louis Sullivan, the Field Wholesale Store (fig. 41) was "a monument to trade, to the organized commercial spirit, to the power and progress of the age." Clearly, this was a

41. H. H. Richardson, Marshall Field Wholesale Store, Chicago, 1885–87. Demolished. (*The Inland Architect* 12 [October 1888]; courtesy of the Art Institute of Chicago.)

building Richardson's peers recognized as a crystallization of urban commerce.

If the Field Store was the clear expression of its age, Marshall Field himself was no less a product of the economic history of the United States after the Civil War. To understand the building we must know something of the man whose name it bore, and the company he controlled.

Born at Conway, in western Massachusetts, in 1834, Marshall Field arrived in Chicago in 1856 after a boyhood spent in rural New England. His rise in the commercial world began with a clerkship in the wholesale dry goods firm of Cooley, Wadsworth and Company. By 1861 he was general manager, and a year later a partner in the successor firm, which continued to grow, change names, and include as partners men such as Levi Z. Leiter and Potter Palmer. By 1881 the others were all gone, and Marshall Field and Company stood as their successor. Although his initial wealth derived from his mercantile activities, the fortune Field had amassed by the time of his death in

1906 was gained equally if not largely from his speculation in urban real estate in Chicago and elsewhere. The centralization of business downtown which the Field Wholesale Store so clearly represented to the observers of the 1880s meant a boom in urban land values, and men such as Leiter, Palmer, and Field were quick to turn commercial profits into capital investments. Marshall Field personally owned the wholesale store designed by Richardson and the land it rested upon, and leased the building to his company. Nonetheless, Field thought of himself primarily as a merchant, and it is with the company which still bears his name that he is most accurately identified.

During the shifting patterns of partnership in the 1860s and 1870s, the nature of the company changed markedly. The business began as a wholesale firm, but in the course of time it developed a split personality, handling a large variety of goods in two divisions. Retail and wholesale shared the same quarters until 1872 when, in the wake of the Great Fire, the company erected a five-story-plus-basement brick wholesale establishment at Madison and Market (now Wacker). Thereafter the company consisted of two distinct branches, the one with a decidedly local and feminine appeal, the other as clearly territorial and masculine. Retail provided the glamour. It catered to the fashionable ladies of the city. Here woman was queen. Its store on State Street was elegant in decor, with quality goods to satisfy her every desire. Wholesale, on the other hand, serviced the vast territories along the rail network beyond the city limits. Richardson's building served the needs of the traveling man from the outlying district. It was a matter-of-fact space efficiently laid out to expedite the buyer on a short schedule. He would travel to Chicago by night train, debark in the morning at the nearby station, meet the general salesman as he entered the store, establish his credit, proceed from department to department where he found wares neatly but simply displayed, make his selections, arrange for shipment, and return to his hometown at the end of the day. There was little need for the elegance surrounding the impulse buying over on State Street.

We now think of Field and Company as a fashionable retail department store; in fact, in the 1880s, wholesale did five times the annual business as retail. It was for this major, masculine branch of the company that Field invited Richardson to provide both shelter and symbol. That Richardson succeeded we learn from Sullivan who, in his *Kindergarten Chats* of 1901, called the store "a rich, sombre chord of manliness . . . [which shows] when and where architecture has taken on its outburst of form as a grand passion. . . . It refreshes and strengthens, because it is elemental, bespeaks the largeness and the bounty of nature, the manliness of man." Sexing buildings was a favorite pastime of nineteenth-century architectural critics, but Sullivan's words here accurately reflect the image projected of the wholesale branch of Marshall Field and Company in the 1880s.

The year 1881 saw more than the formation of Marshall Field and Company. By May, Field had acquired the entire (half) block bounded by Adams, Franklin, Quincy, and Fifth (now Wells) streets in the Loop, a single property he had put together over a period of time from fifty-one separate lots (fig. 42). Already in January the *Chicago Tribune* reported that Field's purchases in the block had "started again the old story that a new site is being selected for Field & Leiter's wholesale store," but, as the lease on the old property at Madison and Market would not expire until 1889, Field took his time about building at the new location. It was not until April 1885 that he asked Richardson to design a wholesale store. Although the newspapers continued to report Field's lack of hurry as late as October, in fact, once the project got under way, it moved along as rapidly as possible. Richardson's preliminary studies must have been made during the spring and summer, and by August he needed the exact site mea-

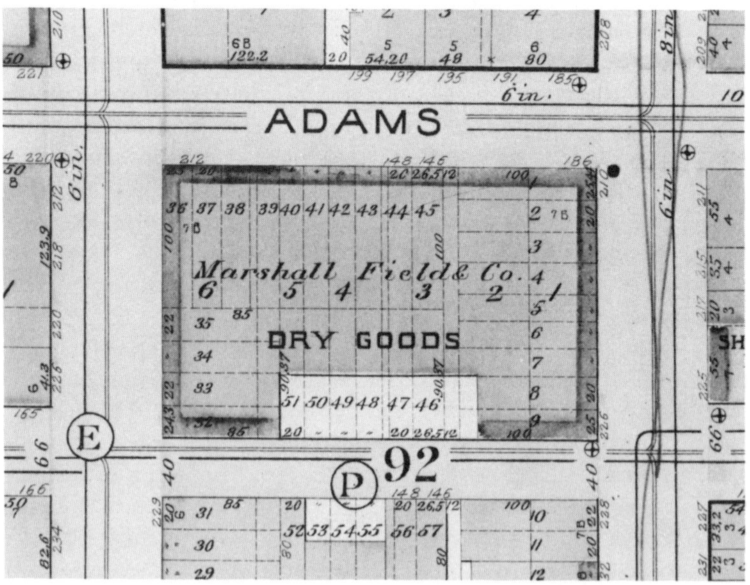

42. Field Store, plot plan superimposed on an atlas of Chicago. (From *Atlas—Chicago Central Business Property,* 1891; courtesy of the Chicago Historical Society.)

surements necessary to prepare working drawings. By October, in fact, Field was ready to unveil his plans, sign a contract for construction, obtain a building permit, and begin excavation.

On 11 October 1885 Richardson was staying at the Grand Pacific Hotel, one block east of the site of the proposed wholesale store. From there he wrote his son that he hoped the contracts would be signed in the next day or two. He must have been interviewed by a reporter from the *Tribune* at this time, for that newspaper on the twenty-fifth ran a description of the project. The reporter could have learned only from Richardson himself that "beauty will be one of the objects aimed at in the plans, but it will be the beauty of material and symmetry rather than of mere superficial ornamentation. H. H. Richardson, the famous architect . . . has long had certain ideas which he wished to embody in such a building. . . . It will be as plain as it can be made, the effects depending on the relations of the 'voids and solids'—that is, on the proportion of the parts." A look at the drawings convinced the reporter "that the structure will be a distinct advance in the architecture of buildings devoted to commercial purposes in this country." The same article informed the public that Norcross Brothers had contracted to build the building. By December the foundations were in and the stonework of the exterior walls was under way, but labor troubles associated with the Haymarket Riot of 1886 delayed occupation of the building until June 1887, more than a year after the architect's death. (It was quietly demolished in 1930 and replaced by a parking lot.)

Richardson designed a U-shaped block rising seven stories above a basement (roughly 125 feet). The total square footage of about 500,000 more than doubled that of the old wholesale facility at Madison and Market. The plan provided at ground level a glass-covered loading dock occupying an indentation in the center of the Quincy Street side of the building. The interior was separated into three large rooms by fire walls running north and south, extending the side walls of the indentation to the Adams Street front. The rest of the plan was subdivided into bays by the structural grid; the necessary services were concentrated along the Quincy Street side. Many of the details of the structure remain unclear, but it does appear that there were two basic column types. Those from the basement through the third floor were intended to be of iron with terra-cotta fireproofing, according to surviving drawings; those of the fourth through the seventh floor were to be of wood. Existing photographs of the interior suggest that this division of materials was actually carried out. The use of structural wood in a building of this size and importance caused some Chicago observers to question its ability to resist fire, a central concern in a city that had witnessed the blaze of 1871. But Field had twice experienced the destruction by fire of his retail store, and there can be little doubt that this was an important consideration of the building program. The fire walls and the terra-cotta cladding for the iron columns have been mentioned among other fireproofing measures. The wooden construction above the third floor was also designed with fire resistance in mind. The upper structural system seems to have been a modified version of "slow-burning" or "mill" construction used in New England textile plants. This system employed widely spaced heavy timbers carrying a solid oak floor which, because of their size alone, resisted rapid consumption by fire. Field was a dry-goods merchant from New England; he did business with New England textile mills. He certainly knew about slow-burning construction. More importantly, perhaps, so did Richardson's Brookline neighbor and erstwhile client, Edward Atkinson. Atkinson was an extraordinary individual who as a fire insurance executive sought to promote traditional fire-resisting technology through pamphlets and articles. One illustrated article appeared in *Century Magazine* in February 1889. In it Atkinson sets slow-burning construction against what he calls "combustible architecture," writing in part that "the art . . . is little known outside . . . of New England." His first illustration is of the Marshall Field Wholesale Store, which he describes as a "most conspicuous example of the right method of dealing with timber and plank in a commercial warehouse, . . . the motive of the plan having been derived from the customary method of constructing a textile factory." The Wholesale Store, he adds, is nothing "but a glorified cotton factory." We shall return to this remarkable allusion when we consider the sources of Richardson's exterior design.

Viewed from any position on the three major streets in front of the building's three main facades (Franklin, Adams, Fifth), the structure loomed up as a massive stone block. Early observers were struck by its size and by the dimensions of some of its stones. Its scale overwhelmed. Adjectives such as "enormous," "massive," "palatial," "huge," "Cyclopean," "immense," and "mammoth" were routinely used in nineteenth-century descriptions. Individual stones in the battered granite base were unequaled in size anywhere else in the city. Those used in the sills of the first-floor windows, judging from photographs, must have approached eighteen feet in length. The load-bearing outer walls were of brick fronted by rock-faced Missouri red granite from the sidewalk to the belt course at the level of the second-floor windowsills, and cut East Longmeadow red sandstone above that, although Richardson and Norcross apparently buried structural metal in the first-floor window heads and elsewhere in the stonework. The building originally had a ruddy exterior although it darkened rapidly, and in descriptions by Sullivan and others it was often said to be brown. Existing black-and-white photographs are equally deceptive; there exists a preliminary perspective sketch which perhaps best suggests the monochromatic blush of the original block.

The stone of the ground floor was laid up in courses of equal thickness except for a narrow band at the height of the windowsills. Above, the pattern of sandstone was layered ashlar of alternating narrow and broad courses, a favorite of the time for the architect. At several points in the height of the arcades the horizontality of the block as a whole was reinforced by interrupting the dominant pattern with continuous horizontal lines. Echoing the narrow band at the height of the ground-story sills were (1) the dressed belt course at the top of the granite base; (2) an interruption of the alternating courses by a thick course of stone carrying the horizontal line of the recessed spandrels between the second and third, third and fourth, and fifth and sixth floors; (3) the band of squared stones occupying the area of the arch spandrels at the level of the fourth story; (4) the continuous sill of the seventh floor; and (5) the leafy cornice and parapet capping the whole. Such painstaking attention to detail produced the remarkably high quality in the collaboration of Richardson and Norcross.

The facades are world famous. We recall from the *Tribune* article that the relations between solids and voids were the architect's chief concern. In the rough granite base a horizontal basement slit was topped by a broad, segmentally arched opening divided into a triad by mullions and transoms. Floors two, three, and four were bound together by the main arcade stretching thirteen bays on Adams and seven on Franklin and Wells between broad corner piers. The windows within each arch at levels two and three were coupled and double hung; the arched opening at the fourth level contained triplets of which the center only was a double-hung vent. Floors five and six were also joined by an arcade of twice the number of arches as the floors below; the upper arches were grouped in pairs centered upon the larger, lower arches. Each opening contained one double-hung sash. Groups of four rectangular openings marked the top floor, and turned the vertical thrust of the lower arches into a horizontal terminus marked by the cornice. All sashes were set at the inner face of the walls to expose their maximum thickness and enhance the sense of mass projected by the entire structure, a sense in no way compromised by decorative accents such as the corner boltels or the occasional carved capital. Since, as we shall see, this pattern of solids and voids was not new to this building, it was by its sense of quality and its projection of concentrated and controlled power that the Field Store achieved its place in the history of urban architecture.

Richardson did not establish an original pattern of solids and voids in his design of the main facades of the Field Store. In fact, there had been a number of recent examples he might have studied. Wheaton Holden pointed to Peabody and Stearns's R. H. White Warehouse in Boston (1882–83) as a probable source; Donald Hoffmann nominated John W. Root's McCormick Harvesting Machine Company Building (1884–86), erected just two blocks west of the

43. George B. Post, Produce Exchange Building, New York, 1884–86. Demolished. (Courtesy of the New York Historical Society, New York.

site of the store; and a host of commentators have cited another source as the model for Richardson's design as a whole. The correspondence between the Field facades and those of George B. Post's Produce Exchange Building (1884–86) in New York is indeed astonishing (fig. 43). The store and the Exchange were so close, and the Exchange so well published, that there can be little doubt that Richardson knew Post's building. Indeed, the possibility is strong that Richardson sought to improve upon this model. Writing of the Exchange in *Century Magazine* for August 1884, Van Rensselaer criticized the building in such a way as to bring to mind Richardson's subsequent design for Marshall Field. "Take away in imagination the story above the cornice . . . suppress the utterly superfluous and disturbing tower; forget the unfortunate porches and the crude ornamentation, and we have a structure which is very fine in general proportion, and in the shape, sequence, and contrast of strong and even noble features." In this context, the Field Store looks like an attempt to apply Van Rensselaer's criticism to a similar building program; on the other hand, it is possible to speculate that Van Rensselaer is here echoing some of those thoughts Richardson told the reporter of the *Chicago Tribune* in October 1885 he had "long . . . wished to embody in such a building."

Those ideas were, in fact, gathered from a wide variety of sources, ancient as well as modern, and tested by the architect in several previous commercial works. The source most frequently cited for the exterior is the Florentine palazzo of the quattrocento, whether it be the Strozzi, the Medici-Ricardi, or the Pitti. The connection is indeed direct. Both Field (in 1875, at least) and Richardson (in 1882) had visited Florence, and the equation of the modern merchant prince with his Medician ancestors has been made too often to need elaboration here. The connection is direct, but not convincing. The early Renaissance palazzo is clearly divided by pronounced belt courses into three horizontal layers of approximately equal height, the lower of which is usually more closed and more heavily rusticated. This produced, even in the Pitti, which is roughly equal in overall height to the Field Store, a radically different treatment of solid and void relationships, not to mention a radically different scale. Richardson certainly had in mind the image of the Florentine palazzo (witness his use of the boltel from this source) but he essentially altered that image in adapting it to his program.

On his continental trip in 1882 Richardson not only looked at the buildings of the Romanesque and Renaissance, he visited and admired other stone-arcuated structures that have a bearing on the

44. Gridley J. F. Bryant (?), Commercial Street block, Boston, 1857. (Photo by the author.)

Field facades. He collected photographs of the Pont du Gard near Nîmes and the Roman aqueduct at Segovia, as well as other lithic monuments. Both are impressive in size, in the size of their voids, and in the size of their individual building blocks. They presented the architect with examples of the scale and the powerful masonry forms brought under control that were evident in the Field Store. Richardson certainly drew upon these and many other European models when he came to consider the Field facades, but he drew upon other more cogent sources from his own early experience as well. Montgomery Schuyler is explicit in citing those mid-century granite commercial structures that must have caught Richardson's attention as an undergraduate, some of which, however modified in design and use, still line the Boston waterfront (fig. 44). In the discussion of the Field Store in his *American Architecture,* Schuyler observed that Richardson told him "that there was more character in the plain and solid warehouses that had been destroyed [in the Boston fire of 1872] than in the florid edifices by which they had been replaced," and went on to observe that "in the [Field] warehouse . . .

Mr. Richardson himself resisted this besetting temptation . . . and his work certainly loses nothing of the simplicity [of those Boston granite models designed by Bryant and others] . . . but emphasizes it by the superior power of distributing his masses." One specific granite structure must have attracted Richardson, although it stood on Beacon Hill rather than by the harbor (fig. 45). The Beacon Hill Reservoir, erected in 1849 behind Bulfinch's State House, was a massive stone basin articulated by tall round-headed arches and topped with a machiolated cornice of a type Richardson was to study and restudy before he or his successors rejected it for the store. We have no direct evidence that Richardson admired the reservoir, but we do have the characterization of it by a contemporary that suggests that in the 1880s it was viewed in terms we now apply to the architect's mature work. Writing in the *Memorial History of Boston* (1880), Charles A. Cummings thought it "the noblest piece of architecture in the city . . . absolutely free from excess or effort or affectation—its cyclopean masonry unvexed by details and unbroken save by the simple order of round arches." He labeled it "the most striking example of the right use of granite . . . [and] a perpetual reminder to every thinking architect . . . of that quality in which our architecture is most deficient,—the quality of repose." Surely Richardson, who was

45. Beacon Hill Reservoir, Boston, 1849. Demolished. (From *Gleason's Pictorial,* 1855.)

46. H. H. Richardson, Hayden Building, Boston, 1875. (Photo by Jean Baer O'Gorman.)

often to rely upon the word "repose" to characterize his stylistic intention, could not have overlooked such a prominent and sympathetic local landmark. The reservoir was, indeed, Richardsonian before Richardson.

The architect had begun to apply his study of past stone architectures to the design of urban commercial buildings in the mid-1870s, following those earlier, bookish mercantile works in New York and Springfield. The immediate antecedent to the Field Store in his own work was his design for the Cheney Building in Hartford (1875–76), but it was in another building begun in the same year that he betrayed his connection to the local lithic tradition. In the Hayden Building in Boston (fig. 46), designed for the architect's father-in-law, Richardson began to bind floors together beneath tall arches, although they occur here only at the third and fourth levels. The lower floors are treated as independent units linked by aligned mullions. The ground floor has been altered, but from a preliminary drawing we learn that it was, at least on the narrow Washington Street front, trabeated and divided into three sections. The second floor is opened by a broad segmental arch embracing three windows separated by stone posts. The fifth and top floor is fenestrated differently once again. This is a continuous series of rectangular voids formed of monolithic posts and lintels which echo the structural details of Alexander Parris's shop fronts at Quincy market. This treatment links Richardson's work directly to the Boston granite style. Drawing the unvexed structural expression of stone from the style's early works, Richardson applied the textural surfaces and arcuated detailing of its mid-century exemplars to form the basis of his own urban work. He merged the lessons of the Romanesque, Renaissance, and *Rundbogenstil* with the native urban commercial tradition to give shape to that "quiet and monumental treatment of wall surfaces" that was his basic aim in urban architecture.

So far we have looked only at the principal facades of the Field Store, those along Franklin, Adams, and Fifth. On the Quincy Street side of the building the articulation of the other walls turned the corner but extended just two bays to the indentation occupied by the glass-sheltered loading dock. The walls forming this indentation were handled in a dramatically different manner from the other elevations, although here again we cannot be certain about every detail in the absence of photographs of this utilitarian aspect of the building. They appear (on surviving drawings; fig. 47) to have been walls of exposed brick opened by densely packed, segmentally arched windows. It was the massing of these openings in the sides of the indentation that produced the brightly lighted interior remembered by some former employees. Such a treatment of facade Richardson borrowed from another native source, the same one in which he found his slow-burning construction. The arch-articulated brick mills of Lowell, Lawrence, Manchester, or elsewhere in New England (fig. 48) stand as witness to Edward Atkinson's assertion that the Field Store was nothing "but a glorified cotton factory." In turning from European models to the native commercial buildings of Boston and the mill towns of New England, Richardson was adapting the past to the needs of the New World.

At seven stories the Field Store was average among the structures of the 1880s erected in the center of Chicago, although it would be quickly dwarfed by the "skyscrapers" of the next few years. It contributed nothing technically to the development of the tall office building, but it did suggest a new urban scale. This was in part because of the gigantic size of its individual stones, frequently commented upon, but another element becomes apparent as we study Chicago streetscapes of the early 1880s and glance at the plot of fifty-one lots assembled for the site of the wholesale store by Marshall Field (fig. 49; see also fig. 42). Chicago's blocks were made before the mid-1880s of irregular groups of individually designed buildings producing the kind of additive composition or design by accumulation characteristic of the contemporary architectural scene in general. Field in his real estate transactions and Richardson in his approach to a building as a whole—not a sum of parts—produced a coherent pattern embracing a full block (see fig. 41). This would become immediately commonplace in urban commercial design, but in the mid-1880s it represented a grand and simple gesture which made the store stand out "amidst a host of stage-struck wobbling mockeries," to quote Louis Sullivan's picturesque phrase. As late as the 1920s the store could still impress the keen observer this way. The architect Rudolf Schindler wrote to Richard Neutra from Chicago in 1921 that Richardson "places in the middle of the ugly cities large monumental square buildings which appear like meteors from other planets." He could have had only the Marshall Field Wholesale Store in mind.

In the center of the main or Adams Street facade, at ground level, the row of segmental openings was scarcely interrupted by a single entry marked below by three shallow steps, and above by a peaked lintel inscribed, simply, MARSHALL FIELD. That was all that was needed to identify this as a commercial center. Sullivan's friend and mentor, the architect and socialist John Edelmann, saw this when he wrote that the building was a "grim fortress of trade . . . a

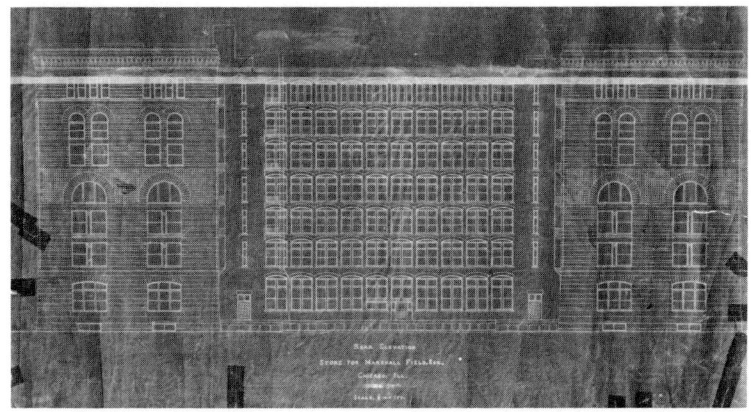

47. Field Store, blueprint after a working (?) drawing of the Quincy Street elevation, 1885–86 (Courtesy of the Department of Printing and Graphic Arts, Houghton Library, Harvard University.)

48. Mill building, Gloucester, Massachusetts, ca. 1900. Although this probably postdates the Field Store, it represents a decades-old type. (Photo by Jean Baer O'Gorman.)

huge square box with regular ranges of openings for light—massive, simple, brutal, naive, a true expression of its inward character." Such a contemporary reading of the building's form is astonishingly apt connotatively as well as denotatively. On one level the building suggested its mercantile content by reference to commercial antecedents from the Renaissance onward, but it communicated at other levels as well. In the 1880s, an era the economic historians tell us was one of falling wholesale prices, companies generally sought to expand business and consolidate capital. The store was erected to house a trade expanding outward along the railroads into the developing western territories by a man personally identified with the company now

49. Michigan Avenue, south from Jackson Boulevard, Chicago, 1887. (Neg. no. ICHi-04450; Courtesy of the Chicago Historical Society.)

completely under his control. May we not see this expansion of trade reflected in the mammoth size, the blockbuster presence of the building? And this consolidation of capital expressed in the coherent form imposed upon it by Field's real-estate transactions and Richardson's design decisions?

The impact of the building goes even beyond this. It is, finally, a visual analogy, an icon, signifying the capitalist system which created it. According to Geoffrey Broadbent, Charles Pierce defined an icon as a "physical thing, possessing certain 'characters' which it shared with its object. There are 'likenesses' between them and it is these likenesses which enable the one to act as the sign for the other." The fact that in semiotics this concept causes trouble need not concern us. What does apply is the fact that it is possible to find definitions of capitalism written by economic historians whom we assume never heard of the Marshall Field Wholesale Store which read almost as if they were descriptions of the store written by architectural historians. In 1935, for example, Jerome Davis wrote that capitalism is "the economic system under which production, distribution, and finance are becoming concentrated into *large-scale interrelated units,* which are, on the whole, organized into corporations, privately owned, and controlled by a minority, who run them for *private profit*" (my emphases). Such a definition of the economic system under which it was designed and erected elucidates the ultimate meaning of the Field Store, and incidentally suggests an important reason for its continued ranking among the paradigms of world architecture. For the "private profit" of Marshall Field, H. H. Richardson adapted a host of historical images to create a memorable design of "large-scale interrelated units." In so doing he consciously or unconsciously created a capitalist icon. The Marshall Field Wholesale Store was unmistakably an urban commercial house that free enterprise built.

5 • *Ruralism*

He had supposed it to be a natural object.
Frederick Law Olmsted

The compact commercial cores generated by the economic forces of the 1880s, and made manifest in a building such as the Marshall Field Wholesale Store, had their centrifugal counterparts in the outlying satellite towns, bedroom suburbs, and rural retreats that sprang up in the post–Civil War years. Here urban forms would have been out of place. Here Richardson was forced to mine a different, actually in part a nonarchitectural tradition, in his search for the expressive diversity he, following Olmsted, thought appropriate to American society. His solutions in the realm of residential design are among his most refreshing creations, and this is in part because they are free of the humdrumness of repeated historical forms. In mature wooden works he employed the shingle style. In works like the R. T. Paine House in Waltham (see fig. 61) or the E. W. Gurney House at Pride's Crossing (see figs. 62, 63), both places satellites of Boston and both buildings of 1884, natural forms often replace expected architectural details so that glacial boulders or irregular, quarried stones are piled into an overall geological imagery. Nowhere is this more evident than in the gate lodge Richardson added in 1880 to Langwater, the F. L. Ames estate at North Easton, Massachusetts (see figs. 56, 57). Only in the occasional work of A. J. Davis (who himself in his preface to *Rural Residences* [1837] drew a sharp distinction between urban and rural architecture) such as the gate house he designed in the 1850s for Llewellyn Park in Orange, New Jersey, do we find precedents for such natural forms within American architecture. We must look outside the history of building to understand fully Richardson's rural achievement.

Our starting point is the epigraph on the title page of Van Rensselaer's monograph on the architect, a work written by one friend and sponsored by two others: F. L. Olmsted and Charles Sprague Sargent. This epigraph echoes the voice of nineteenth-century New England, Ralph Waldo Emerson. It is that assertion from Emerson's essay "Art" (1841) that beauty will not be legislated, nor repeat in America its foreign history. "It will come, as always, unannounced, and spring up between the feet of brave and earnest men." The epigraph stops here, but the essay itself continues for several more lines, ending with the admonition that "it is in vain that we look for genius to reiterate its miracles in the old arts; it is its instinct to find beauty and holiness in the field and roadside, in the shop and mill." Here was Emerson's call for an American cultural independence, for new art forms based upon new sources of inspiration. Obviously Van Rensselaer and Olmsted thought this applied to Richardson. In the Field Store he had sought part of his inspiration in the "shop and mill"; in his rural works he looked to the field, to the land, for his "new and necessary facts." In "The Young American" (1844) Emerson wrote that "the land is the appointed remedy for whatever is false and fantastic in our culture. The continent we inhabit is to be physic and food for our mind, as well as our body. The land, with its tranquilizing, sanative influences, is to repair the errors of scholarship and traditional education, and bring us into just relations with men and things."

To sing the song of nature and proclaim an organic theory in the arts were, of course, not original to Emerson or to any American. R. P. Adams and others have reminded us that the roots of both extend to Coleridge and beyond. But Emerson and his followers put such immigrant ideas to the service of an indigenous culture. They naturalized them in the same way A. J. Downing naturalized English picturesque sources in his *Treatise on . . . Landscape Gardening, Adapted to North America* (1841). These writers required that inherited cultural forms be influenced by American conditions, American sites, American materials. In "Self-Reliance" (1841), for example,

Emerson asked, "why need we copy the Doric or the Gothic model?" and went on to suggest that "beauty, convenience, grandeur of thought and quaint expression are as near to us as to any, and if the American artist will study with hope and love the precise thing to be done by him, considering the climate, the soil, the length of the day, the wants of the people, the habit and form of government, he will create a house in which all these will find themselves fitted, and taste and sentiment will be satisfied too." It is a commonplace that both Louis Sullivan and Frank Lloyd Wright responded favorably to Emerson's plea, or perhaps that plea as recharged by Whitman, but they both recognized in Richardson a precursor (see chapter 7) who had accepted the same challenge, with, however, inchoate results because he died early, leaving them to finish what he had begun.

This is not to say that Emerson envisioned any of the works of Richardson, Sullivan, or Wright. He had no well-defined program, least of all a specific architectural program. Gothic was to him a natural architecture, as, according to the "forest theory" of its origins, it conformed to organic principle. He admired it, but not as a source of inspiration. But Emerson was, in his own words, "an opener of doors for such as come after," and Richardson, Sullivan, and Wright were certainly Emersonian "come-afters." In the suggestiveness of Emerson's ideas, or his ideas filtered and broadcast by others, Richardson and his descendants found a fertile field for speculation.

America's search for identity in the years after the revolutionary period focused on the land, which was after all the only strictly American element in the culture. As Norman Foerster put it in the first sentence of *Nature in American Literature* (1923), "since the early white settlers of America were Englishmen, who brought with them and later imported the culture of the Old World, for a long time the distinction of America, the newness of the New World, was simply nature." Interest in the land was political (Manifest Destiny) and scientific as well as artistic; in fact, it was hard to separate out its constituent components. Thomas Cole's *Ox Bow* (1846), a view of an incipient crescent lake on the Connecticut River near Mount Holyoke, Massachusetts, was painted fifteen years after the publication of Charles Lyell's *Principles of Geology* (1830–33), that science's first mature synthesis in which the earth-forming dynamics of wind and water were given primacy. American poets, painters, scientists, and politicians all turned in the first half of the nineteenth century to the American landscape, for whatever diverse reasons, as the source of inspiration. As Emerson wrote in "Nature" (1836), "we nestle in nature, and draw our living as parasites from her roots and grains."

The discovery of America by Americans reached its climax in the "era of exploration" following the Civil War, as the railroad bound West to East and the search for mineral riches became intense. This era is distinguished by the unrivaled land forms that were revealed beyond the one-hundredth meridian by geologists, painters, and photographers, who flooded the East with a plenitude of astonishing images. Reacting to these new images, Emerson in "The Young American" observed that "the nervous, rocky West is intruding a new and continental element into the national mind, and we shall yet have an American genius. . . . I think we must regard the *land* [his emphasis] as a commanding and increasing power on the citizen, the sanative and Americanizing influence, which promises to disclose new virtues for ages to come." The new-West imagery enhanced the cause of cultural nationalism by adding supporting visual data to an attitude which had developed in the course of the century. In the Rockies, Yosemite, and Yellowstone were natural forms to rival the man-made landmarks of Europe. One manifestation of this idea is the constant repetition of variations on the theme, found in scientific as well as popular literature, that American landforms were substitutes for European monuments. In one example from the hundreds that could be cited, Samuel Bowles, who was incidentally the brother of one of Richardson's early clients, Benjamin, in *Our New West* (1869) wrote of Yosemite that "'The Cathedral Rocks' and 'The Cathedral Spires' unite the great impressiveness, the beauty and the fantastic forms of the Gothic architecture. From their shape and color alike, it is easy to imagine . . . that you are under the ruins of an old Gothic cathedral, to which those of Cologne and Milan are but baby-houses." Such a passage unites American hyperbole with cultural chauvinism by suggesting that American landforms were "bigger and better" than European architectural monuments.

Another aspect of this usage is found in the names "Cathedral Rock" and "Cathedral Spires." Here we have that tradition of naming natural formations after the architectural types they suggest. This, too, is hardly American in origin, but in nineteenth-century America, and especially in the popular coverage of the opening of the West, it became a common, almost a central theme, the theme of nature's architecture. And if nature could imitate architecture, architecture could certainly imitate nature. It seems possible to suggest that an Emersonian follower of Olmsted, such as Richardson was, might indeed be taken with the idea of turning the architectural image in nature into the geological image in architecture.

Richardson would have known about western discoveries merely by being alive in the 1870s and 1880s, or through the circle of New England intellectuals who were his mentors, clients, and friends. It also seems credible to suggest that a man proud of his descent from Joseph Priestly would have taken at least a passing interest in the sciences at Harvard. He might have on occasion listened to the charismatic Louis Agassiz, father of glacial theory, perhaps even taken some notice of the opening of the Agassiz Museum at the college in 1858. Richardson's friend, Henry Adams, developed a lifelong interest in geology under Agassiz in the 1850s. Later, Richardson's collaborator and environmental mentor, F. L. Olmsted, acted as a direct link to the West. He had worked at the Mariposa Mine in California and had become involved in the preservation of Yosemite, Yellowstone, and Niagara. The work at Yosemite brought him into direct association with Clarence King, a follower of both Agassiz and Ruskin, a survey geologist when Olmsted met him, later a leader of the Fortieth Parallel Survey, author of *Mountaineering in the High Sierras* (1870s), and first director of the U.S. Geological Survey. He was also a man who employed photographers on his western surveys and in such vanity publications as his *Three Lakes* of 1870, with its frontispiece by Timothy O'Sullivan. There seems to be no evidence of a direct connection between King and Richardson, but the geologist was a warm friend of John La Farge and, more importantly, a bosom companion of the Henry Adamses and the John Hays. Adams visited King during the Fortieth Parallel Survey, and King responded with occasional visits to the Adamses in Washington during construction of Richardson's Hay and Adams houses. Whether Richardson knew King or not, however, he could no more have been ignorant of the new-West imagery than we, a century later, can be innocent of the map of the moon or the color of Mars.

The workings of Emerson's land-based cultural inspiration and the ubiquitous new-West imagery first surface in Richardson's career with his design for the Oakes and Oliver Ames Monument erected, appropriately enough, in southeastern Wyoming (see figs. 50 and 55). On 27 February 1873 Oakes Ames, member from Massachusetts, sat in the seat in the House of Representatives at Washington he had occupied for a decade, and listened while his colleagues condemned him for alleged acts of bribery in attempting improperly to influence other members by offering them stock in the Credit Mobilier of America at a price below par. After the vote, it is said, many of them crowded around his chair to explain their ballots as acts of political expediency. Just over two months later Ames died in disgrace, surrounded by his family and friends at North Easton, Massachusetts.

So ended the career and the life of a remarkable and still controversial nineteenth-century manufacturer, politician, and capitalist who had a major role in the creation of the transcontinental railroad. That thin belt of wood and iron would bind East and West into a unit upon its completion in 1869 just as the outcome of the Civil War had rebound North and South just four years earlier. As the partner of his brother, Oliver, in the operation of the highly successful Ames Shovel Company of North Easton, Oakes had entered Congress in 1862, the year in which it granted the Union Pacific Railroad its first charter. By the end of the war no track had been laid, although a limited liability construction company, the Credit Mobilier, had been established in 1864. During the next five years, until the driving of the golden spike at Promontory Point, Utah, where the Union Pacific locomotive bumped "buffalo catchers" with that of the Central Pacific, the Ames brothers and their New England colleagues gradually gained control of both the railroad and the construction company. Oliver served as acting president of the line from 1866 and as president from 1868 to 1871, after which he continued to sit as a director until his death. Oakes assumed personal responsibility for constructing the road in 1867 and continued to direct the flow of capital into the process. Some of that capital came from his congressional peers, and that eventually led to his censure in 1873.

The consensus of history sees that censure as a politically useful act growing out of the election campaign of 1872. In this history merely echoes Oakes's friends and family, who at the earliest possible moment sought to counteract the effects of censure by memorializing the man. At North Easton in 1879 his children began the construction from the design of Richardson of the Oakes Ames Memorial Hall, publishing on the occasion of its dedication in 1881 a long refutation of the charges brought against their father years earlier.

The Ames Memorial Hall, an example of the lingering picturesque Romanesque within the architect's oeuvre, celebrates Oakes as a leading citizen of North Easton; his career as railroad builder was memorialized in a more fitting form in a more fitting location. Meeting in Boston on 10 March 1875, the Union Pacific stockholders requested the directors of the line, who included Oakes's brother and his son, "to take measures . . . for the erection, at some point on the line of the road, of a suitable and permanent monument" to Oakes Ames, "in recognition of his services in the construction of the Union Pacific Railroad, to which he devoted his means and his best energies." The intent was clearly to reaffirm the corporation's belief in Oakes's innocence, and it was probably for that reason that the

50. H. H. Richardson, Ames Memorial, Albany County, Wyoming, 1879–82. (Photo by Jean Baer O'Gorman.)

project languished while a suit against the Credit Mobilier to recover "illegal" profits supposedly resulting from the scandal wound its way up to the Supreme Court. On 9 January 1879 that body handed down an opinion which in effect vindicated Oakes, and at the end of the year the commission to design the monument entered Richardson's office. Construction began in September 1880, and the memorial, now commemorating the recently deceased Oliver as well as his brother, was dedicated in October 1882.

Although Richardson might have chosen to memorialize Oakes Ames's reputation as railroad financier by a monument incorporating realistic depictions of him, his brother, engines, and tracks (an intrusive and perhaps ultimately ludicrous object within its intended setting), he opted for a generalized form which, in Emerson's phrase, "nestles in nature." The relief heads of Oakes and Oliver by Augustus Saint-Gaudens are incidental within the overall mass. The site selected was at the summit of the Union Pacific line, a spot near Sherman Station in the Wyoming Territory between Cheyenne and Laramie (fig. 50). With both line and station now removed, the location is a high, lonely, windswept, vast, and barren meadow dotted in summer with colorful wildflowers. The site is animated by the shifting lights and shadows of scudding clouds and framed by spectacular geological formations. Visible to the distant south and west are the

51. Wood engraving after S. R. Gifford, Pilot Knob, California. (From W. C. Bryant, ed., *Picturesque America,* 1872–74.)

Rocky Mountains dominated by Long's Peak; and to the north, the Laramie Range; and, to quote F. V. Hayden's description of the area in *Sun Pictures of Rocky Mountain Scenery* (1870), "in the intermediate space are groups of lower peaks, or cones rising like steps to the higher ranges." Richardson's pyramidal stone monument was clearly designed and erected to echo at scale the rich formations of the divine architect or his scientific handmaiden, geology. But, serene and silent amid this continental landscape, it is at once appropriate for its site and clearly a work of artifice; it is based on both geometry and geology; it is both man-made and mountain.

Almost certainly Richardson never saw the site, never in fact traveled west of St. Louis or Chicago. Olmsted, who had crossed the West, might have relayed its natural wonders, and Norcross, who took a crew of skilled workmen from Massachusetts to Sherman to erect the monument, might have described the location, but the one would have been too general and the other too late. When in 1880 Richardson came to design the monument, he needed a concrete conception of the place. He needed visual images from which to work in order to create the shape he did, so he must have turned to that flood of new-West imagery reaching the eastern seaboard from beyond the one-hundredth meridian. It was to be found everywhere, from government scientific reports to expensive limited-edition photographic portfolios, to the illustrated popular press, to "coffee-table" publications, to stereographic cards. A coffee-table production such as the two-volume *Picturesque America,* edited by William Cullen Bryant and issued in 1872–74, contains hundreds of views of both eastern and western landscapes, including examples of "nature's architecture" spread from the coast of Maine to the coast of California. Therein Richardson or an assistant might have found inspiration in the boxwood engraving after a view designed by S. R. Gifford of Pilot Knob in northern California (fig. 51). Although the site is far more dramatic than the high meadow at Sherman summit, and the magnitude of the Knob larger than the monument, the correlation in profiles between the two forms seems too close to be a mere coincidence.

Yet the characteristics of the high meadow itself seem to have inspired the shape of the monument, so it is doubtful that the architect would have relied specifically upon Gifford's view of the California Knob. He could have learned about the area around Sherman by turning to other pictorial sources, especially ones generated by the construction of the Ames's Union Pacific itself. The photographer A. J. Russell issued, in 1869, *The Great West Illustrated,* an album of fifty views taken in the vicinity of the line as it snaked its way westward from Omaha across southern Wyoming and on to Promontory. Certainly this album was available to Richardson through his clients, the Ameses. These photographs record both the works of man as he bridged canyons and leveled hills and the works of nature to be found along the route. In these contrasting views the works of man seem frail and transitory; perhaps, in reaction, Richardson sought to create a man-made form seemingly as permanent as the natural forms it conventionalizes. Plate 6 of the *Great West* ("Skull Rock") is especially attractive in this regard (fig. 52), not only because it is a startling pyramidal formation of weathered granite that Russell describes as "situated three miles south of the Railroad, in the mining district of Dale Creek Canon," which was just west of Sherman Station, but also because, according to Hayden's *Sun Pictures,* also illustrated with Russell's photographs, it was one of the "granitic ruin-like piles that give the peculiar distinction to the plateau surface of the Laramie Mountains"; that is, to the area around Sherman (see fig. 50).

The photographs in Russell's album were but a small selection of those he took of the Union Pacific between 1867 and 1869. The remainder were known, however, at least in New England, from the "Illustrated Course of Lectures . . . [on the] Scenery Between Omaha and San Francisco taken . . . for [the] Union Pacific Railroad" given throughout the Northeast during the 1870s by one S. J. Sedgwick, who seems to have gained control of Russell's negatives. "Skull Rock" does not appear by name in the catalog of Sedgwick's stereographic cards, although "High Rocks, near Sherman Station" does, but there were in his list at least three views of another outcropping, "Reed's Rock," which he describes as "a pile of granite about a quarter of a mile west of the station [at Sherman] and within a stone's throw of the tracks, rising from the ground as clean and regular as though built by man" (fig. 53). Surely, here was inspiration for monumental design!

Richardson's intention to use geological references at Sherman summit cannot seriously be questioned. Olmsted, in a letter to Van Rensselaer after the architect's death, wrote that he "never saw a monument so well befitting its situation, or, a situation so well befitting the special characteristics of a particular monument. . . . [It is]

52. A. J. Russell, "Skull Rock." (From *The Great West Illustrated,* 1869; reproduced by permission of the Huntington Library, San Marino, California.)

53. A. J. Russell, "Reed's Rock," 1869. (Courtesy of the Union Pacific Historical Museum, Omaha.)

on the peak of a great hill among the great hills. . . . A fellow passenger [in the Union Pacific car] told me that . . . it had caught his eye . . . [but] he had supposed it to be a natural object. Within a few miles there are several conical horns of the same granite projecting above the smooth surface of the hills. . . . At times the monument is under a hot fire of little missiles driven by the wind. But I think they will only improve it."

That ornamental forms in architecture ought to derive from nature was a commonplace of nineteenth-century aesthetic theory, but even John Ruskin, the writer most closely associated with the tenet, did not propose the idea in isolation. He is at pains, in fact, in *The Seven Lamps of Architecture* (1849), to recognize a duality in the creative act. At the beginning of the "Lamp of Power" he asserts that "whatever is in architecture fair or beautiful, is imitated from natural forms; and what is not so derived . . . depends for its dignity upon arrangement and government received from human mind." This duality of nature and geometry, or what Ruskin himself calls "gathering and governing," recognizes art—and architecture—as not merely real but ideal, as not merely the product of imitation but of cultivation as well. Other nineteenth-century writers on ornamental art provide us with processes for idealizing nature. In *The Grammar of Ornament* (1856), for example, Owen Jones proceeds from the principle that "true art consists in idealizing, and not copying, the forms of nature." He includes among his many propositions two of special interest: number 8, which asserts that "all ornament should be based upon a geometrical construction," and number 13, which says that "natural objects should not be used as ornaments, but conventionalized representations founded upon them sufficiently suggestive to convey the intended image." That Jones writes of floral ornament need not detain us, for his principles could be adapted to larger forms as well. Ruskin and Jones are quoted here because Richardson included their books in his working library.

If Richardson did indeed "gather" in the photographs of A. J. Russell or others information about the geological imagery at the site of his monument, he modified these images by "governing" them, by imposing a geometrical order upon revealed natural form. He may even have taken a cue from a passage in Hayden's *Sun Pictures* in which these "massive piles, like the ruins of old castles . . . scattered all over the summit" are described geologically as "once angular masses, probably nearly cubical blocks, and they have been rounded to their present form . . . by exfoliation. Nature seems to abhor all sharp corners or angles." Richardson, we might suggest, reversed the process of nature by creating his monument as an angular reshaping of the weather-beaten granite piles he found in A. J. Russell's photographs. He might even have been aware that the abrasive effects of windblown debris would eventually soften the monument lines, as Olmsted observed in his letter to Van Rensselaer. And he must have thought of the conventionalized natural form of the monument as emblematic of the merger of man and nature.

There is every reason to suppose that Richardson agreed with Owen Jones's principle of conventionalized nature. He had been educated to rational, geometric planning at the Ecole, and often during the 1870s, as at Trinity, where as we have seen the plan is based on a series of squares, organized architectural forms according to regular shapes. The Ames Monument is said to measure sixty feet in plan and rise sixty feet into the air. It is, then, contained within a cube, one of the perfect solids. Ruskin had already recognized the power of such simple solids when he recommended a "choice of forms approaching to the square [and in three-dimensions, the cube] for the main outline" of a building. But not only the salient dimensions herald the monument as artifice. Richardson and his builder took great pains to construct it from local granite, but they cut that granite into dressed shapes and laid them in regular patterns. There is a base course of massive blocks from which the pyramid rises, its battered walls offset midway to the truncated apex. Below the offset the stone is rock-faced random ashlar, above, rock-faced horizontal ashlar. The offset itself is marked by four smooth-faced "shoulders" at the four corners resting upon two thin, continuous layers of stone. The monument, then, was constructed with the same exquisite sense of scale and attention to detail that marked the Field Store and Norcross's other works for the architect.

Whether or not such a process of "gathering and governing" as suggested here occurred on the drawing board in Richardson's Brookline office, that is exactly what happened at the site near Sherman summit. The Ames Monument was actually erected from stones "gathered" by quarrying Reed's Rock and "governed" by shaping and dressing (fig. 54). The natural formation some seventy feet high was removed from the landscape and reshaped by Norcross's workmen to create the new, conventionalized, granitic outcropping dedicated to the memories of Oakes and Oliver Ames. It is no wonder, then, that this man-made mountain appears among the *Marvels of the New West* published by William M. Thayer in 1887 (fig. 55).

54. Reed's Rock, Albany County, Wyoming, 1882. "Quarrying" for the Ames Monument is about to begin. (Courtesy of the Union Pacific Historical Museum, Omaha.)

55. The Ames Monument. (Wood engraving after a photograph published in William M. Thayer, *Marvels of the New West,* 1887.)

Following the design of the Ames Monument in 1880, Richardson produced a series of houses for suburban or rural sites in the satellite areas of Boston. For these residential designs he seems to have extended and modified the creative process based on natural imagery he had learned for the monument. Since these eastern sites offered no stiff competition from neighboring geological forms, as was the case at Sherman summit, he could afford to relax the "governing" aspect of the equation and permit his designs to evolve easily out of their inspirational sources. In no case do we have the architect's own statement of his intentions. With the Ames Monument we can speculate about his aims on the basis of site, available relevant source materials, and the indirect witness of Olmsted. With the Ames gate lodge and the Gurney and Paine houses we have only the works themselves and their extraordinary analogies to images in nature to guide our reading of Richardson's rural work. This visual evidence, coupled with the Emersonian association established by the epigraph on the title page of Van Rensselaer's monograph, seems convincing.

The gate lodge at North Easton, designed in 1880, fronts an estate landscaped by Olmsted for F. L. Ames (fig. 56). The building combines a bachelor's residence with a gardener's potting shed, joined by the polychromatic arch over the entrance road. The plan flows freely across the green, rural site. The walls are piled glacial boulders punctuated by dressed stone. The whole is quieted by the fluid, orange-tile roof spreading its sheltering eaves and horizontal ridge above the animated stonework. Characteristically, the mature architect relied for his architectural effect on the natural colors and textures of stone, the interplay of man-made and natural forms, the contrast of textures, solids and voids, and the harmonious integration of building and environment. He also relied on geological imagery. The detailing of windows, arches, and walls makes little reference to architectural history. Window jambs and heads are split stones; the archway of the wellhead is primitively composed of split voussoirs (fig. 57); the *objet-trouvé* stones of the walls were shaped by geology, not man. It is as if Richardson had adapted to the needs of a building with essential roof and openings the image of an outcropping, a geological shape of a kind he may have known from Russell's *Great West* (see fig. 52). But there are other natural images that come to mind as

56. H. H. Richardson, Ames gate lodge, North Easton, Massachusetts, 1880–81. (Photo by the author.)

57. Ames gate lodge, exterior detail. (Photo by the author.)

we look at the relationship between the main archway and the site, images such as the painting by David Johnson of Virginia's Natural Bridge (1860), a familiar eastern monument of nature's architecture (fig. 58). That Richardson might have known the original oil is doubtful: he was more likely to have known the image from its reworking in Bryant's *Picturesque America* or other such popular source. There is in North Easton another monument which seems to stem from a source such as Virginia's Natural Bridge, Olmsted's Civil War Memorial in front of the Ames Memorial Hall (fig. 59). This is a landscaped hillock penetrated by an archway of crude stonework more reminiscent of paintings of the Natural Bridge by Frederic Church (1851; fig. 60) or John Henry Hill (1876) than by David Johnson.

Whether Richardson or Olmsted had a specific natural image in mind, both certainly had aimed at an association with nature's architecture. Both drew inspiration not from architectural history alone but from natural history as well. Here were images born of the

American land; here was architecture, to paraphrase Emerson, that nestled in nature and drew its meaning from her roots and grains.

At the R. T. Paine house in suburban Waltham, a design of 1884, for the man who had chaired the building committee of Trinity Church, Richardson merged the shingle style with the geological image (fig. 61). The generous site was a lofty and wooded one landscaped by Olmsted. The house is located at the top of the rise to provide a southward vista toward the distant commercial center. The architect's work here consisted of a huge addition to an older mansarded house moved to the new location. The contrast between the existing fabric, so like the architect's early houses for himself and Dorsheimer, which he ignored, and the addition was the measure of Richardson's development as a designer. The shingled elevation facing the approach road incorporates a Palladian window in recognition of the eighteenth-century roots of the shingle style. At ground level and toward the view the external material turns into granite boulders glacially shaped and piled by the builder into low walls and rounded towers. Architectural detailing is elemental, as in the primi-

58. David Johnson, *Natural Bridge,* 1860. (Courtesy of Reynolda House, Museum of American Art, Winston-Salem, North Carolina.)

59. F. L. Olmsted, Civil War Memorial, North Easton, Massachusetts, 1881–82. (Photo by the author.)

60. Frederick Church, *Natural Bridge*, 1852. (University of Virginia Art Museum; gift of Thomas Fortune Ryan.)

tive arch at the salient angle of the house. Heads, jambs, and sills surrounding openings in the glacial wall are roughly split slabs of contrasting stone. On the side toward the view Olmsted provided a terrace formed by low, serpentine, boulder walls. These echo the towers and sweep house and site into one consistent whole. Architect and landscapist here collaborated to interweave architecture and environment into one geological image.

61. H. H. Richardson, R. T. Paine house, Waltham, Massachusetts, 1884–87. The glazed bays between the stone towers at left are later additions. (Photo by William H. Pierson, Jr.)

62. H. H. Richardson, E. W. Gurney house, Pride's Crossing, Massachusetts, 1884–86. Altered. (Courtesy of the Boston Athenaeum.)

And finally, for Henry Adams's brother-in-law, Ephraim W. Gurney, Richardson designed in 1884 a summer house at Pride's Crossing on Boston's North Shore (fig. 62). The site is back from the coast but high, the house emerging from the granite ledge overlooking the sea. Although now densely wooded, the original land, as old photographs show, was barren. A vista of rock and sky met the approaching eye. Richardson placed the house near the top of the ridge, its irregular features composed of sloping roofs and locally quarried granite walls. There is little overtly architectural detail on the exterior. The windows have no jambs; lintels and sills are rough monoliths split out of a local quarry (fig. 63). Newspaper accounts at the time it was first occupied describe the house as "built of rough stones with their moss on, and present[ing] a most picturesque and unique appearance." The external walls seemed the work of "nature's trowel," to borrow a phrase from Thomas Hardy. The house extended the natural stone base as if it were another outcropping photographed by A. J. Russell. It is an architecturally interpreted, or conventionalized, landform. It was Richardson's final effort at geological imagery, at an American rural architecture in sympathy with the American land.

In the Field Store Richardson, at the end of his life, developed an archetype for American urban commercial architecture based upon his merging the historical stone architectures of Europe with New England industrial and mercantile prototypes. In the Ames gate lodge he gave definition to an American rural architecture founded upon and thus harmonious with regional land forms. For the passengers speeding between city and suburb in the 1880s, he was to provide physical manifestations of stasis and shelter in a series of railroad depots. With the small-town library, this was his final contribution to the shaping of an American society as defined by Olmsted in his lectures of 1868 and 1870.

63. Gurney house, exterior detail. (Photo by the author.)

6 • Commuterism

Two or three may be styled commuters' [rail]roads, running chiefly for the . . . city business-men with suburban homes.

The Atlantic Monthly, 1865

The commuter railroad depot appeared as a characteristic design problem after the Civil War as the centrifugal suburbs became bedrooms, and business began to pile up in the burgeoning commercial centers. The railroads then became what the highways have since become: the thin threads connecting the two halves of commuter life. "Commuter" itself was coined in the United States around 1870, according to the *Oxford English Dictionary,* to denote a person who traveled by rail at a reduced rate (i.e., using a commutation ticket) between two points, usually *urbs* and suburbs.

The depot was programmatically a point of transference on this transportation circuit leading from rural or suburban home to downtown office (or shopping) and return. It was the place where passengers changed from carriage to train or from train to carriage. It provided a sheltered double funnel connecting two modes of transportation along a continuous line. The requirements of this program were simple: establish a point of stasis along a line of movement; provide shelter during moments of transition; and supply basic services such as general or segregated waiting areas, men's and women's rooms, ticket and telegraph office, and baggage room. Larger stations might offer additional services, such as a dining room or an agent's quarters.

In the series of commuter depots stretching westward from the Hub that the mature Richardson designed during the 1880s for the Boston and Albany Railroad, whose vice-president was his old Harvard chum, James Rumrill, the simplicity of this program dictated a direct architectural response. These depots were crystallizations of the duality of transition and shelter, of flux and shadow. On one side of the enclosed waiting area the roof reached out over the carriage entrance as a porte cochere to gather commuters into the interior; on the other side sheds broadened out horizontally above the trackside platform to convey them warm (or cool) and dry into the waiting train. Traffic flow beneath this generous umbrella was simple and direct: from carriageway to entrance to waiting room past ticket window to train (and vice versa):

suburb ________/‾‾‾‾‾‾‾‾‾‾‾‾‾‾‾________ city
(home) ⟷ carriage ⟷ shelter ⟷ train ⟷ (work; shopping)

As J. H. Phillips wrote in *Architectural Record* in 1914, Richardson "held very properly that rural way stations were not for show. Ostentation . . . was to be avoided. Their chief purpose was to provide comfortable and pleasant shelter for passengers. . . . Accordingly, they were designed with simple, wide overhanging roofs, and broad platforms on all sides while the substantial walls of local stone gave an air of permanence and stability."

When these depots were located in a town or village, as at Holyoke or South Framingham, the architect avoided the usual clock tower, such as that marking the otherwise largely Richardsonian Boston and Providence terminal by Charles Brigham at Stoughton, Massachusetts (1888), in favor of an understated, horizontal silhouette. The result is that "quiet and monumental" treatment characteristic of all the architect's major work. Where the depots were located in rural surroundings, he created in them subtle reflections of the local environment. Roof lines are ground-hugging, either horizontal repetitions of flat terrain or sloped echoes of declining ground between carriage lane and lower railroad track. Walls are of regional rock left rough-textured and often articulated by contrasting belt courses and window surrounds. Here too a tower would have been out of place.

This marriage of architecture and site extended beyond the buildings themselves into their surroundings, a fact that generated much of the early writing about them. As he did so often in his career, Richardson frequently collaborated with F. L. Olmsted to provide suitable settings for his commuter depots, especially those of the Boston and Albany line. The result, again to quote Phillips, was that the "charm of the stations . . . has been greatly enhanced by the admirably designed surroundings. These stations were given ample grounds, laid out with pleasant surfaces of turf, ornamented with diversified shrubbery disposed in masses and in such a way as to give most pleasing impressions." This attention to quality in both buildings and landscaping can be explained only by reference to a last, least tangible requirement of the building program for a commuter depot in the 1880s: that is, the two-faced image it was intended to project of the railroad on the one hand and the community it served on the other. *Engineering Magazine* in 1891 recognized that "nothing advertises a road better than tasteful station buildings; nothing helps attract and build up local traffic more quickly." On the other hand, both Phillips and the magazine *Garden and Forest,* edited and largely written by Richardson's friend and neighbor C. S. Sargent, who not incidentally became director of the Boston and Albany line in 1880, recognized the value of the road to the suburb. In answer to its own question whether there could "be a better advertisement for a suburban neighborhood than a station and grounds" like those at Chestnut Hill, *Garden and Forest* stated that "they imply refinement, good taste and a regard for the amenities of life in the local community." It went on to congratulate the Boston and Albany for having the good business sense to provide buildings and grounds which "are the best of their class in the world." And according to Phillips, when "the question of a new station for one of the Boston suburbs arose, the . . . editor [of the local newspaper] urged upon the directors of the railroad that . . . the station and its surroundings be given an artistic character, expressing the standing of the suburb as a progressive and cultivated community." Another contemporary observer called the depot "the town's official entrance."

The commission for the earliest of the Boston and Albany depots, for Auburndale, entered Richardson's office in February 1881, shortly after Rumrill assumed the vice-presidency of the line. This was the first depot on the new commuter circuit established by the road as an addition to its "main line" freight and passenger service to Springfield, the Hudson River, and beyond. Richardson produced at Auburndale (fig. 64) his definitive solution to the building program,

64. H. H. Richardson, Boston and Albany Depot, Auburndale, Massachusetts, 1881. Demolished. (After Van Rensselaer, *Henry Hobson Richardson and His Works*, 1888.)

and O. W. Norcross translated his design into a superbly executed building, facts we learn only from photographs, drawings, and early descriptions, as the building itself was pulled down long ago. The centrally located ticket and telegraph office and toilets divided the long rectangular plan into men's and women's waiting areas. A baggage room occupied one end. Only the angular bulge of the ticket booth at trackside interrupted the four straight walls of granite ashlar trimmed with red sandstone around broad rectangular openings. This lithic prism huddled beneath an oversized hip roof covered with slate and edged with terra-cotta. A squat stone chimney barely broke the horizontal line of the ridge. An arched eave marked carriage access beneath the generous overhang supported by square-sectioned wooden posts which flowered into gently curving brackets. The interior displayed paneling of vertically grooved boards and exposed brick. The interest of the railroad and its architect did not end with the building itself, as Olmsted provided the landscape setting. The result, according to *Garden and Forest,* afforded "the traveler a pleasant, verdurous prospect whichever way he may turn his eyes." The type established here was to be repeated with variations in other locales but never essentially altered.

A second depot, at Palmer on the main line, was commissioned in August 1881. It varied the type by being larger, thus containing a dining room and offices in a second level under the roof. It also served two lines, the Boston and Albany and the New London and Norwich, which crossed here at an acute angle, hence the trapezoidal plan. This site too was landscaped by Olmsted. The station remains in a state of precarious neglect. One of Richardson's masterpieces of the type followed Palmer, the Old Colony depot designed for his North Easton patrons, the Ames family, in the fall of 1881 (fig. 65). This is his clearest scheme, his neatest crystallization of flux and shelter as the essentials of the building program. His preliminary study shows traffic patterns from porte cochere to central entry, into the lobby, then right or left around the ticket office into men's or women's waiting rooms, and finally out through broad openings to the trackside shed. The definitive plan retained this direct, divided flow while it reduced the perimeter to a basic rectangle. The divided traffic pattern is captured in three dimensions by the five low arched openings in the granite elevations, one defining the carriage porch, the remaining four in pairs opening the waiting areas to Olmsted's landscaping beyond. Another glance at Richardson's preliminary sketch for the depot (fig. 66) demonstrates his emphasis on the horizontally extending hip roof hovering over the granite walls as actual and symbolic shelter. The weight of the pencil lines captures graphically this emphasis, with more pressure applied at the skyline. Broad dormers and a squat chimney at the ridge enhance the spreading character of the low structure, which is carried beyond the waiting area itself by the long sheds parallel to the track. In the building erected by Norcross, the deep overhangs are supported by straight, diagonal struts braced against the sturdy walls. Carved animals lurk beneath the roof of the porte cochere, on the arms of the benches at trackside, and on the transoms of the arched windows of the waiting rooms. They are whimsical elements of decoration taken from medieval vocabulary and characteristically subordinated to the geometric control of the larger architectural forms.

Emphasis on the basic elements of architecture is once again evident: on roof as shelter, on geometric masonry as decoration, on the celebration of site as formal inspiration, on the play across space of basic load-bearing forms such as the arch of stone and the brace of wood. The Old Colony ranks with the Ames gate lodge and the Marshall Field Wholesale Store as one of Richardson's finest moments.

A second triumph followed after a year's break. The Boston and Albany depot at Chestnut Hill, commissioned in April 1883 and no longer extant, again varied the type without essentially altering

65. H. H. Richardson, Old Colony Depot, North Easton, Massachusetts, 1881. (Courtesy of the Boston Athenaeum, gift of Mrs. Harrison Schock from the estate of Frank I. Cooper.)

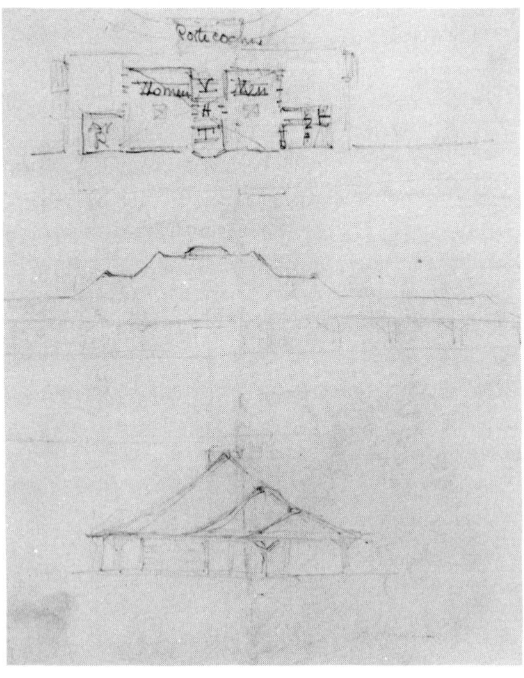

66. Old Colony Depot, preliminary study. (Courtesy of the Department of Printing and Graphic Arts, Houghton Library, Harvard University.)

the effect (fig. 67). The broad sandstone-lined arches reappeared flanking the porte cochere beneath a double-sloped slate roof which has reminded more than one observer of the salt-box silhouette of the seventeenth-century New England farm house. Covered walks on the opposite side of the station led down to a shed at the level of the tracks where they flared outward at an awkward angle. These ground-paralleling eaves and the traditional silhouette wedded building to site. So did Olmsted's landscaping. *Garden and Forest* called attention to the ensemble in 1889: "Several fine trees ornament the grounds, including . . . White Pine . . . a clump of old White Willows . . . and a symmetrical American Beech that stands in the centre of the lawn opposite the carriage entrance. . . . In other directions . . . masses of foliage border the grounds. On the other side of the track, as at Auburndale, is a narrow strip of grass, edged with trees and hardy flowering shrubs, and everywhere these masses are neither stiffly arranged nor scattered without purpose, but carefully grouped so as to secure variety in unity, interest, grace and harmony." What Rich-

67. H. H. Richardson, Boston and Albany Depot, Chestnut Hill, Massachusetts, 1883. Demolished. (After Van Rensselaer, *Henry Hobson Richardson and His Works,* 1888.)

ardson and Olmsted joined in "grace and harmony" at Chestnut Hill in 1883 only a demolition crew could pull asunder around 1960.

The year 1883 saw the erection of two more way stations, that for the Connecticut River Railway Company at Holyoke and the Boston and Albany's at South Framingham. Both follow the larger, two-story type which first appeared at Palmer. Although the site at South Framingham precluded an extensive landscape scheme by Olmsted, here too Norcross carried out Richardson's design (fig. 68). The plan is a long rectangle originally chiefly occupied by a general waiting room (the building has been converted to a restaurant) that rises vertically to the underside of the cross-gable roof. The ticket office at trackside and the monumental stone and brick fireplace opposite established the cross axis, but the most dramatic feature of the space is the exposed trusswork overhead. The oblong plan rises into a stone prism capped by a low hip roof of slate. Walls of gray granite set in random ashlar with red mortar are trimmed in red sandstone. Openings are broad, rectangular, mullioned, and transomed. A continuous horizontal eave surrounding the stone block extends out to the shed supported by wood piers and curved brackets at trackside, and a protective roof supported by curved brackets over the entrance

68. H. H. Richardson, Boston and Albany Depot, South Framingham, Massachusetts, 1883. (Photo by Cervin Robinson for HABS, Library of Congress.)

69. H. H. Richardson, Boston and Albany Depot, Woodland, Massachusetts, 1884. (After Van Rensselaer, *Henry Hobson Richardson and His Works,* 1888.)

at roadside. The trackside shed is repeated by a free-standing one of wood on the north side of the tracks. Above the deep overhangs of the roof on the north and south sides rises a second stone story in the form of three gables. The larger, central one encloses a segmental window lighting the waiting room; the smaller, flanking gables contain squat Palladian windows. In the valleys between the gables are decorative accents: large carved stone lion's heads. A small eyebrow dormer looks out from the eastern slope. All in all, the South Framingham depot is a larger variation on the Richardsonian commuter building established at Auburndale.

In the year between July 1884 and July 1885—the architect's last July—the Boston and Albany commissioned no fewer than five stations, at Brighton, Waban, Woodland (fig. 69), Eliot, and Wellesley Hills, all on the Boston side of South Framingham. With the exception of Brighton these were small "flag" stations, a couple no more than one room and a roof. The slope of that roof at Brighton continued down to join the lower level of the tracks. An eyebrow window offered light to the gloom beneath. Waban sported a ticket bulge at one corner, and to go above it a rounded eave resting upon shaped brackets. Again the eyebrow dormer watched over the tracks. The Woodland station is half roof, a high hip, and half wall. Toward the tracks sheltered outdoor waiting areas within the bulk of the block flanked the ticket window. Eliot was a close variation of Woodland. Wellesley Hills doubles the conformation of Waban. The rounded corner ticket bay reflects an opposite bulge for baggage. As at Brighton a sloping roof links the higher waiting room to the lower tracks. Of these five stations only those at Woodland and Wellesley Hills survive, the one a derelict, the other a victim of unsympathetic conversion to commercial use.

The series of suburban commuter depots designed by Richardson (a series carried on admirably after his death by his successors, Shepley, Rutan, and Coolidge) were perceived by contemporary observers as they have been by historians as a distinct and highly influential achievement in railroad architecture. "It is almost needless to explain," explained *Garden and Forest* (i.e., Charles Sprague Sargent) in its 1889 article on Auburndale, "that until Richardson began to build rural railroad-stations none had been erected in America which deserved much consideration as intelligent and pleasing works of art. . . . The best of our small country stations were plain, cheap structures, looking no more like stations than like buildings of some different kind, while the average varied between grotesque and fragile attempts at picturesqueness of aspect and shabby make-shifts disgracing the very name of architecture. We had vulgar little stations that looked like exaggerated kiosks, and brick and wooden boxes which merely displayed the railway company's desire to expend as little money as possible. . . . When the Boston and Albany Railroad Company asked him [Richardson] to design their station at Auburndale he showed for the first time what such a building ought to be." We no longer take such a jaundiced attitude toward architecture before Richardson, but we can still appreciate the influence Richardson's architecture in general, and his designs for railroads in particular, had on the work of his contemporaries. As in all his mature buildings Richardson created in his stations a reassuring sense of belonging and lasting which must have appealed to the postwar generation. By reducing at Auburndale and elsewhere the elements of the problem to a minimum of shelter and flux, then quietly celebrating these elements with simple and solid design, Norcross's execution, and Olmsted's gracious grounds, Richardson produced a fresh vision of the commuter depot which was to be reflected not only in the many Richardsonian stations erected all along the westward flow of the railroad system but also in the mature work of his creative successors, especially that of Frank Lloyd Wright.

The flow of humanity outward from the urban centers along the commuter lines came to rest in the satellite towns whose gateways were the railroad depots. For these outlying towns and rural sites Richardson, as we have seen (chapter 5), designed expressive domestic establishments. He also applied his disciplined formative talents to another suburban building program characteristic of the time and place. The small town library or, better, community cultural center, as many contained not only books but art collections, museums of natural history, and lecture spaces, reflected the flowering of popular education in this country in the second half of the nineteenth century. They also served as memorials to men who had helped build small-town America after the Civil War.

We have seen (chapter 2) the formal evolution of the Richardson library beginning with the eclectic composition for the Winn Memorial in Woburn, Massachusetts, and progressing through the Ames Memorial at North Easton to the Crane memorial at Quincy (fig. 70). On 20 February 1880, Albert Crane of New York offered the town south of Boston a library to be dedicated to his father, Thomas

70. H. H. Richardson, Crane Memorial Library, Quincy, Massachusetts, 1880–82. (Photo by Wayne Andrews.)

Crane, a Manhattan dealer in Quincy granite. The Crane family picked the architect, perhaps on the recommendation of Charles Francis Adams, Jr., chairman of the building committee, and brother of Richardson's friend Henry. The building, dedicated on 30 May 1882, represents the architect's definitive solution to the problem, and so ranks with the Field Store, the Ames gate lodge, and the station at North Easton or Chestnut Hill at the top of his achievement. It should be emphasized, especially here, that the achievement was a formal one. As working libraries the Crane and other memorials were hopelessly backward. They were designed, as libraries had been since the Renaissance, as gentlemen's studies, with tiered alcoves surrounding a high paneled reading room. In the 1870s this obsolete approach had been replaced by the metallic bookstack separated from the public, and this was what the new American Library Association advocated for library design. Through the 1870s and 1880s the ALA attacked one Richardson design after another as old-fashioned and expensive, and created for effect rather than efficient use.

In his search for compact, coherent form Richardson was fortunate that the program for the Crane Memorial called for neither gallery nor museum, although early studies do incorporate stacks and lecture hall. In the final plan only alcoves and reading room flank the entrance leading to a central circulation desk. A stairway to the left of the entrance rises to the librarian's apartment on the second level. Richardson's studies for the external mass also show a characteristic process of simplication from which the final tightly controlled form emerged. The plan of the building as built is a long rectangle interrupted by the indentation at the entry and the bulge of the stair tower. Above this rises a gabled three-dimensional stone mass, the silhouette contained by vertical walls and horizontal ridge emphasized by tiles. The front gable and the stair tower are fully embraced by this envelope. The tripartite horizontal organization developed for the alcove wings of the Winn and Ames memorials is repeated here, and reiterated in the water table, belt courses, and row of eyebrow dormers that enrich the slope of the roof without interrupting its continuity of surface. Here as in other mature works Richardson has managed to indicate on the exterior the arrangement of spaces within: the clerestory lighting the alcoves, the large mullioned and transomed window marking the reading area, the cavernous archway signaling entry, the stumpy tower suggesting vertical circulation, and the triple-arched window of the gable opening into the apartment beneath the roof. Historical detail is present, but only to accent this otherwise elemental design. At the Crane Richardson achieved his definitive library; later ones at Malden or Burlington show a lessening of the control reached at Quincy.

Richardson died at forty-seven, in mid-career, his work far from complete. Against the full sweep of architectural history, his achievement downtown must appear tentative if measured by the career of Louis Sullivan or the course of the Chicago School, and his suburban domestic, railroad, and library architecture must be judged at tentative if measured against the fully articulated organic architecture of Frank Lloyd Wright. As unfinished as it was, however, its significance was clear. As John Hay suggested in his eulogy of 1886, and as the German writer Leopold Gmelin, among others, made explicit in 1899, Richardson was "the founder of an independent style of architecture in the new world." Whether he consciously or unconsciously sought to fulfill Olmsted's wish for appropriate and therefore diverse architectural forms for city and country, Richardson achieved works in which he reached the stature of that "American genius" Emerson was looking for in "The Young American" essay of 1844. We must now consider the influence that American genius had upon the shaping of an American architecture in the works of some of those who came after.

7 • Legacy

L'effort de rénovation se retrouve jusqu'en Amérique, où F. L. Wright, après Richardson, travaille à retrouver des lois bienfaisantes.

André Lurçat

Historians have tracked the influence of H. H. Richardson's work as far afield as Australia in one direction and Britain, Holland, Germany, and Scandinavia in the other. European observers especially, but not exclusively, and above all the Germans, recognized at the time of his death that he had accomplished what no other American architect had ever accomplished. He had, in effect, turned the tide of cultural influence which, at the beginning of his career, was running westward from Europe. He was the first New World architect to have a broad and lasting effect upon the Old World. His legacy was global in scope.

The purpose of this interpretation of H. H. Richardson's work, however, has been to define his contribution specifically to the architecture of late nineteenth- and early twentieth-century America, and it is his influence upon his countrymen that concerns us here. That legacy was multiplex in keeping with the variety of expressive means Richardson developed for a variety of design purposes. There was, of course, the "Richardsonian Romanesque" stemming from Trinity Church and other works, which impressed itself upon the American city of the

71. McKim, Meade and White, Public Library, Boston, 1887–95. (Photo by Jean Baer O'Gorman.)

end of the century, to a degree more apparent before the urban renewal blitz of the 1950s than it is today (see fig. 40). The revived Romanesque was quantitatively Richardson's most important legacy, and his name will forever be associated with it, but qualitatively it must shrink before his more significant gifts.

Through his assistants, especially Charles F. McKim and Stanford White, Richardson was also to affect what has come to be called, with little justification, the American Renaissance. Richardson had drawn from his French training the principles of rational planning and disciplined design while eschewing its classical forms. The next generation accepted these forms as well. McKim's Boston Public Library of 1887–95, a cornerstone of the revival in America, owes much to Leon Battista Alberti, to Henri Labrouste, to Christopher Wren, and to other European sources, but it is in its own classical garb a worthy and completely natural successor to Richardson's Marshall Field Wholesale Store as well (fig. 71; see also fig. 41). The discipline Richardson imposed upon the picturesque was logically extended by some of his followers into the neoclassical revival. Where he had tried to adapt traditional stone architecture to specifically American imagery, McKim and his fellow travelers sought to express American architecture as a culmination of a continuous classical tradition.

A third aspect of Richardson's influence upon his followers brings us to the heart of his achievement. Richardson's focus upon the elemental aspects of architecture appealed to those of his followers who were not seeking an alternative to picturesque composition or a classical renewal, but an architectural means of expressing contemporary American life. These were the architects of the Middle West, and especially Chicago, site of his last great accomplishments in urban design, the Field Store and the Glessner house. The leaders in this search for a fresh American form were Louis H. Sullivan and Frank Lloyd Wright, and of the two it was the younger Wright who profited more from Richardson's legacy.

What did Wright think of his predecessor? Richardson's name appears occasionally in Wright's numerous writings and, given his psychological makeup, it is not surprising that these references reveal his lifelong ambivalence concerning Richardson's memory. In 1908 Wright wrote of the architectural scene he had entered in the 1880s that "the fine art sense of the profession was . . . practically dead; only glimmerings were perceptible in the work of Richardson and of [John Wellborn] Root." Such a statement reflects Wright's intense dislike of those who make architecture merely a business, yet in 1939 and again in 1949 he accused Richardson of having been primarily concerned with getting the job, of putting business before art. This is, of course, false, and Wright in old age may have confused Richardson with Richard Morris Hunt, but this is not the only instance of Wright playing Indian giver to Richardson's memory.

In 1914 Wright paid Richardson the highest tribute of which he was capable when he wrote that his predecessor had touched upon "an organic architecture for America," but he took that back in 1949, saying that "the buildings the firm [of Adler and Sullivan] did were seldom far along the road of organic character until they were compared with the buildings of the robust Romanist [*sic*] in 'rock-face'—H. H. Richardson. Richardson was the grand exteriorist and what a commotion *he* created." Finally, in a single book, *A Testament* of 1957, Wright both admitted "admiring" Richardson and said in another context that he was "just what America deserved most but should have had least—a powerful romantic eclectic." Repeatedly to return to Richardson's memory in this way, like a dog worrying a bone, Wright must have felt a gnawing sense of indebtedness to his predecessor's work.

To understand Wright's ambivalence we must conclude that this was indeed the case but that he hated to admit it even to himself, and this is consistent with what we know of his ego. It is also true that most of these references to Richardson occur in discussions of Louis Sullivan, whom Wright called his *Lieber Meister,* and in these instances there is a ring of jealousy in Wright's remarks. Thus, in *Genius and the Mobocracy,* Wright's characteristically egocentric tribute to Sullivan, we read: "Nor did I ever hear [Sullivan say] a good word for any contemporary of his unless almost nothing for John Root. But later I discovered his secret respect, leaning a little toward envy (I was ashamed to suspect), for H. H. Richardson. Just the same and nevertheless he liked and trusted *me*" (Wright's emphasis). Even in retrospect Wright was loath to give anyone else equal time in Sullivan's attentions.

From remarks written over a lifetime, then, Wright's attitude toward Richardson appears at best guarded, yet, when his ego was not on watch, he could be honest enough to permit credit to fall where it was due, even if that credit was implied rather than stated. In the first edition of *An Autobiography* (1932), Wright ended with a collection of photographs, selected by himself, which was intended to illustrate people who had been of personal importance in his life (the collection was omitted from the better-known edition of 1943). Cecil Corwin, the draftsman who first befriended Wright when he arrived in Chicago fresh from the country, is there, as, on another page, are his influencial uncle, Jenkin Lloyd Jones, his *Lieber Meister,* Sullivan, Sullivan's partner whom Wright so admired, Dankmar Adler, and, finally, in the lower right-hand corner, Henry Hobson Richardson. It should be noted that Richardson is the only one in the group who had not intervened directly in Wright's life. The inclusion of Richardson's likeness in this book demonstrates, more than his contradictory remarks, Wright's recognition of the older man's profound influence on the formation of his own architecture.

Wright, who was twenty and rather a rustic when he arrived in Chicago in the spring of 1887, entered the office of Adler and Sullivan in the fall of the same year. At the same moment three late Richardson buildings were nearing completion in the city: the Field Store, the Glessner house, and, less important here, the Franklin MacVeagh house, commissioned in July 1885. These works by the architect who stood at the top of his profession when he died in April 1886 had a marked effect upon the Chicago of the late 1880s and early 1890s. The example of the completed Field Store caused Sullivan, at about the moment Wright entered his employ, to alter his existing design for the exterior of the Auditorium Building, commissioned in 1886, and later write in his *Kindergarten Chats* (1901) one of the most moving eulogies ever expressed by one American architect for another. In his definitive Auditorium design (fig. 72) Sullivan swept away the picturesque silhouette of his early drawings, reducing the building to a dense block, and borrowed the external relationship between solid and void Richardson himself had adopted for the Field facades. This

72. Adler and Sullivan, Auditorium Building, Chicago, 1886–90. (Photo by Cervin Robinson.)

was but the first of a series of Sullivan projects inspired by Richardson's example. Sullivan's affair with Richardson's work lasted from 1886 until about 1890, and can be characterized as a brief departure from the course he had already set himself in the Troescher Building of 1885, although his definitive Wainwright Building of 1890 was produced only after this episode, and seems to demonstrate a profound understanding of Richardson's achievement. Be that as it may, between the Auditorium and the Wainwright, the office of Adler and Sullivan turned out a series of such specifically Richardsonian buildings as the Standard Club, the Heath house, the Falkenau houses (fig. 73), the Walker Warehouse, and the Anshe Ma'ariv Synagogue, all in Chicago; the Opera House in Pueblo, Colorado; and the Dooley Block in Salt Lake City. In the design of these buildings Wright was, by his own admission, the pencil in his *Lieber Meister's* hand, and, we can add, Richardson was the muse looking over their shoulders.

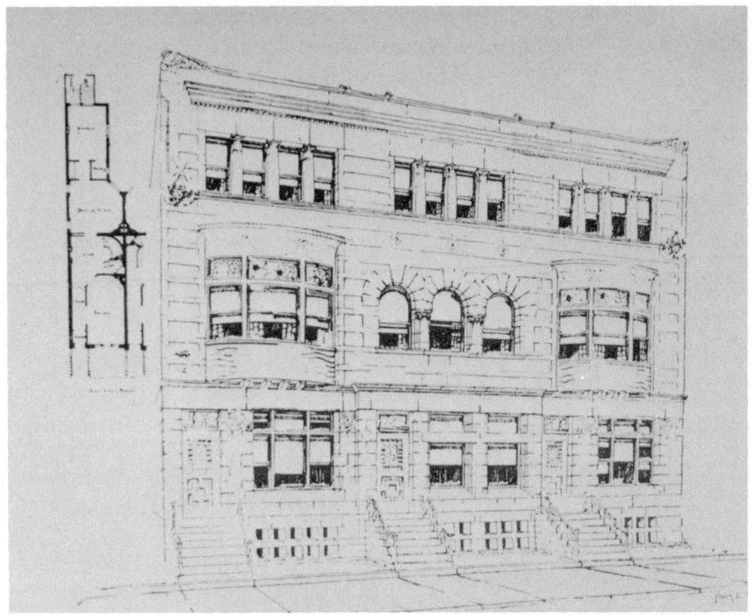

73. Frank Lloyd Wright for Adler and Sullivan, Victor Falkenau houses, Chicago, 1888. (After Manson, *Frank Lloyd Wright,* 1958.)

In the late 1880s, then, Sullivan, the Master, and Wright, the searching neophyte, were saturated with Richardson's work. In *Genius and Mobocracy* the younger man tells of being the only one to understand the Master, of how the two of them would spend long evenings together in the firm's offices, first in the Borden Block and then, after 1890, in the tower of the Auditorium ("occasionally looking out through the romantic Richardsonian Romanesque arches [*sic*] over Lake Michigan"). According to Wright, never one to admit interest in the work of another architect if he could avoid it, Sullivan discussed Wagner, Whitman, Herbert Spencer, or his own writings, but from the context in which Wright reports this, it is clear that the names of Root, a Chicago architect noticeably influenced by Richardson, and of Richardson himself, were also heard in the office. In fact, it is not difficult to imagine Sullivan holding forth late at night upon the merits of the Field Store, forgetting the presence of his apprentice, Wright, just as he seemed to forget that of the student to whom he addressed his tribute to the store in a chapter called "An Oasis" in his *Kindergarten Chats.* "Buildings such as this," he wrote, "and there are not many of them, stand as landmarks, as promontories, to the navigator. They show when and where architecture has taken on its outburst of form as a grand passion—amid a host of stage-struck-wobbling mockeries." Taken as a whole, Sullivan's "Oasis" clearly recognizes the effect the Field Store had on the Chicago urban scene in particular and the development of American commercial architecture in general. Although written long after Wright left him, this probably reflects the kind of praise Sullivan would have had for Richardson's work when, in the late 1880s, he was so much taken with it. And such an intense endorsement of the man and his work by someone he so highly respected at the time must have stimulated Wright to find out for himself what made Richardson's work so worthy of Sullivan's attention.

At the height of their keen interest in Richardson's work, Sullivan and Wright were not limited to the Chicago buildings for inspiration. On 29 May 1888 Houghton Mifflin published in folio Van Rensselaer's handsomely illustrated monograph on Richardson and his work. This is still the basic publication for the study of the architect, but it was also a vehicle for Richardson's influence on Sullivan and especially on Wright. Even though it was issued in a limited edition of 500 copies, and at the rather high price of twenty dollars a copy, it was important enough for Sullivan to acquire it for his own library. Wright probably knew well this and other Richardson titles also in Sullivan's possession. We can picture him alone or with his *Lieber Meister* after office hours, pouring over this volume behind the Richardsonian voids of the Auditorium tower.

Wright's first identifiable designs confirm this study of Richardson. The J. L. Cochrane house in Chicago and the Unitarian Church in Sioux City, both of 1887, the two Hillside houses of 1887–88, and the Oak Park house he built for his new family in 1889, show him to have been an accomplished exponent of the shingle style. In what is probably the earliest evidence we have of his independent existence within the firm of Adler and Sullivan, a signed drawing for the Victor Falkenau houses in Chicago published in June 1888, a little over six months after Wright joined the firm, we see the young draftsman totally submerged in Richardson's example (fig. 73). As has been pointed out more than once, the Falkenau houses are generally Richardsonian and specifically dependent on the Prairie Avenue front of the Glessner house (see fig. 27). The upper rectangular openings divided by fat colonnettes, the basement windows subdivided into lesser squares by plain stone mullions and transoms, and the simple lithic quality of the whole are taken without change from Richardson's just-finished house. Wright's addition of Queen Anne bays at the sec-

74. Glessner house, exterior detail. (Photo by Kevin Harrington; courtesy of the Chicago Architecture Foundation.)

ond floor betrays an overplay by the hand of the beginner, but in all else his indebtedness to his source is direct and obvious.

Sullivan's energies were directed toward the shaping of the emerging tall urban commercial office building, and he naturally focused his attention on Richardson's example at the Field Store. As Wright developed as a draftsman in his office, Sullivan more and more left domestic commissions to his assistant, who thereby early established his presence in the speciality that was to become his career. Sullivan's eye naturally drifted to the Field Store; Wright's just as naturally drifted toward the Glessner house as an appropriate model for his own concerns. The facade of the Falkenau houses records his early reaction to his study of the building. As late as 1949 he, probably unconsciously, recalled this early source of inspiration when he adopted Richardson's design for the service entrance of the Glessner house (fig. 74) for the main feature of the facade of the V. C. Morris shop in San Francisco (fig. 75). The materials have changed but the basic geometry remains the same. The persistence of this detail in Wright's memory suggests the degree of intensity with which he early fixed upon Richardson's domestic example.

Such direct borrowing occurs from time to time in Wright's early career, but he was quick to penetrate the surface effects of Richardson's work, to uncover with Sullivan's guidance the principles that

75. Frank Lloyd Wright, V. C. Morris Gift Shop, San Francisco, 1949. (Photo by Wayne Andrews.)

made that work outstanding. Wright saw Richardson's architecture, as did Sullivan, against the backdrop of the architecture of the 1880s. The picturesque had reached its apogee; buildings were now overrich and unruly assemblages of polychromatic features piled into asymmetrical clusters of splintered vertical masses disputing one another across active voids. Richardson, as we have seen, in his mature work sought a "quiet" architecture, an architecture in which the visual cacophony of post–Civil War building was stilled by formal discipline. Although the surfaces of Richardson's buildings, like those of his contemporaries, sparkle with light, shade, texture, and polychrome, the overall effect is one of control and calm. Both Sullivan and Wright seem to have recognized these characteristics and, in addition, to have come to understand the specific means by which they had been achieved.

76. Frank Lloyd Wright, Winslow house, River Forest, Illinois, 1893, (Photo by Wayne Andrews.)

77. Frank Lloyd Wright, Edwin Cheney house, Oak Park, Illinois, 1904. (After Hitchcock, *In the Nature of Materials,* 1942.)

Between his Richardsonian design for the facade of the Falkenau houses and his Winslow house in River Forest, Illinois, of 1893, the first house Wright later recognized as his own (fig. 76), his progress as a designer careened along an uncertain path. In the Charnley house in Chicago of 1891 he borrowed ideas from Sullivan's Wainwright Building, and in the Blossom house of 1892 Wright dabbled with the colonial revival while lifting his dining room from the Glessner house. But with the Winslow house Wright began to show the effects of his understanding of Richardson's achievement. It is Richardsonian not only in specific details, such as the low-sprung arch of the porte cochere, or in parts of the plan, where Wright again borrowed the Glessner dining room, but more essentially in the organization of the exterior. Here Wright merged images derived from Richardson's depots and his libraries. The exterior is organized into three superimposed horizontal zones: a masonry base rising to a continuous sill beneath an ornamental frieze punctuated with window voids, the whole capped by a simple hip roof. Such a resolution of a building into constituent horizontal layers is evident in the plates of Van Rensselaer's monograph, especially so in the photograph of the alcove wing of the Ames Memorial Library (see fig. 25). Other plates seem to lie behind other early Wright domestic designs. The Edwin Cheney house in Oak Park of 1904, a mature Wright building, has an irregular exterior plan produced by projections and recessions which are, however, gathered in by the all-embracing simplicity of the hovering hip roof (fig. 77). The result is an architecture of quiet and repose, quite like that of Richardson's Woodland Station, a drawing of which also appears in the Van Rensselaer folio (see fig. 69). In the latter, too, the simple, protective roof hovers above the irregular masonry walls, and the front of the depot, in which the ticket window is flanked by deep recessions, is exactly repeated in the front of the Cheney house, where the central bank of glass doors projects out to the edge of the roof between flanking recesses. Wright's characterization of Richardson as an "exteriorist" suggests how he saw the work of the earlier architect. The horizontal organization of the wall and the formative function of the roof were to become hallmarks of Wright's mature work.

As Wright slowly developed his own system of domestic design in the score of years embracing the turn of the century, he drew upon a variety of source materials whose roots penetrated deeply into American architectural history. The works of Thomas Jefferson, the designs of A. J. Downing and A. J. Davis, the shingle style and its antecedents, all mingle in his mature work with more exotic sources, including Japanese and native American forms. Here his early study of Richardson's work has been emphasized, not to diminish the importance of the others, but to focus on Richardson's most important gift to the shaping of an American architecture. As we have seen, Richardson's search for an appropriate language of design led him to a variety of solutions for a variety of problems, and especially in relation to his influence on Wright, it led to an incomplete body of suburban and rural domestic design in which he sought to create what Wright was later to label the "natural house." More than the imitation of detail in his early work, more than an understanding of the principle of disciplined form, Wright gathered from Richardson's work the rudimentary vision of an American architecture expressive of American life because it was inspired by American natural forms. Wright was to call this "organic architecture," and not only create a complete body of domestic work based on the ideal of a harmonious interrelationship between nature and architecture, but articulate a complete theory based on that principle. Here again his sources are multiplex, but the Ames gate lodge, and the Paine and Gurney houses, where specific examples of a natural architecture upon which he could build.

Wright built a whole architectural theory in part using themes expounded in fragments by Richardson. In his 1894 speech, "Architecture and the Machine," the younger architect employed Richardsonian words such as "simplicity," "repose," and "quiet," words that reappear in later writings, especially in the series he called "In the

Cause of Architecture," published in *Architectural Record* in 1908 and 1914. This is Wright's first extended formulation of his theory, and here we have implicit and explicit references to the Richardsonian model. We find echoes of the older architect in statements such as this: "To let individual elements arise and shine at the expense of the final *repose* [my emphasis] is for the architect a betrayal of trust, for buildings are the background or framework for the human life within their walls and a foil for the nature efflorescence without. So architecture is the most complete of conventionalizations and of all the arts the most subjective except music." And we find implied references to Richardson himself in conjunction with "the ideal of an organic architecture." In the introduction to the famed Wasmuth monograph of 1910, Wright describes his prairie house in three groups: "the low-pitched hip roofs, heaped together in pyramidal fashion, or presenting quiet, unbroken skylines; the low roofs with simple pediments countering [*sic*] on long ridges; and those topped with a simple slab." Two of the three have Richardsonian models.

To create an organic architecture, Wright, like Richardson, had to study the images of nature and then conventionalize them; he had to "gather and govern" his sources. In a letter of 1935 describing a trip across the Dakota Badlands, Wright reacted to the wondrous natural forms he encountered there in a way reminiscent of nineteenth-century travelers, surveyors, and explorers such as Samuel Bowles or Clarence King (see chapter 5). "What I saw gave me an indescribable sense of mysterious otherwhere—a distant architecture. . . . As we came closer a templed realm definitely stood ambient in air. . . . Endless trabeations surmounted by or rising into pyramid (obelisk) and temple. . . . Here was the element, architecture, cut of the body of the ground itself. . . ." Wright's was a rather belated recognition of nature's architecture, and a clear confirmation of his theory of organic design. He gathered, and he governed, by imposing an organizing geometry upon his natural materials, using over the course of his long career in design the entire spectrum of geometric figures. Wright's early implementation of these Richardsonian characteristics can be seen clearly in his design of 1902 for the Hillside Home School at Spring Green, Wisconsin (now the drafting rooms of Taliesin East). It rises from the slope of the hill like an outcropping (fig. 78), but an outcropping designed by a geometrician. The Richardsonian elements of round arch and rock-faced ashlar are grouped into a series of rectangular piers rising to the underside of the low, floating hip (fig. 79). Here the Ames Monument merges with the Woodland Station and is transformed by Wright's developed sense of space and

78. Frank Lloyd Wright, the Hillside Home School, Spring Green, Wisconsin, 1902. (After Hitchcock, *In the Nature of Materials,* 1942.)

79. Hillside School, exterior detail. (After Hitchcock, *In the Nature of Materials,* 1942.)

80. Frank Lloyd Wright, Sol Friedman house, Pleasantville, New York, 1949. (Photograph by Ezra Stoller © ESTO.)

proportions. It is clearly a work by the younger man, and just as clearly an extension of Richardson's rural architecture.

It is necessary to emphasize again and again that Wright's references were many, especially over the length of his extended career. Richardson's example was for him one among a host of fruitful lessons, but the influence of the older architect was formative, because early and intense, and later residential designs from Taliesin East of 1914 to the Alvin Miller house of 1946 at Charles City, Iowa, or the Sol Friedman house of 1949 at Pleasantville, New York (fig. 80), despite the changes wrought in family life and the developments in mechanical equipment and structural materials and techniques, are still flavored by the Richardsonian vision. This assertion does nothing to diminish Wright's genius, or to dilute his own even more special contributions to the shaping of an American architecture.

Richardson's premature death left his work incomplete, that is, the work by which his essential contribution to the architectural shaping of an American society should be defined. Downtown, the Field Store showed Louis Sullivan what could be made in expressive terms of a preskeletal urban commercial building; in the suburbs and beyond, the Ames gate lodge showed Wright how nature could be governed in the process of creating an organic architecture. It was Sullivan and then Wright who carried on what Richardson left unfinished, transforming his inchoate vision as they developed their own theories about an architecture for America in their own time.

By seeking to express the developing articulation of American society after the Civil War through a variety of architectural forms, Richardson achieved the position of "first," to quote John Hay, or "founder," to quote Leopold Gmelin, a formative relationship to the achievers of the next generation.

Bibliography

Study of the life and work of H. H. Richardson requires the use of unpublished as well as published sources. The primary collections of manuscript material are those of the Archives of American Art, the papers belonging to the architectural firm of Shepley, Bulfinch, Richardson, and Abbott on deposit at the Houghton Library, Harvard University, and the rich collection of architectural drawings given to that library many years ago. The Loeb Library at the Harvard Graduate School of Design houses the architect's library and collection of photographs.

What follows is a chronological list of significant publications by and about H. H. Richardson from 1871 to the present. It is not intended to be inclusive. For isolated publications of photographs or drawings of individual buildings, see Ochsner 1982. Two abbreviations appear: *AABN (= The American Architect and Building News*) and *JSAH (= Journal of the Society of Architectural Historians*).

1871

Staten Island Improvement Commission [F. L. Olmsted, Elisha Harris, J. M. Trowbridge, H. H. Richardson]. *Report of a Preliminary Scheme of Improvements. Presented January 12th, 1871*. New York, 1871.

1872

Gambrill and Richardson. *Descriptive Report and Schedule for Proposed Capitol Building of the State of Connecticut*. New York, 1872.

Proceedings in Connection with the Ceremony of Laying the Cornerstone of the Buffalo State Asylum for the Insane. Buffalo, 1872.

1875

"The Arts." *Appleton's Journal* 14 (4 September 1875) : 312. (Concerns Brattle Square Church tower.)

1876

"The Report on the New York State Capitol." *AABN* 1 (11 March 1876): 82–83.

Building in Hartford." *AABN* 1 (21 October 1876): 339–41. (See correction, *AABN* 1 [4 November 1876]: 359.)

1877

"Trinity Church, Boston. . . ." *AABN* 2 (3 February 1877): 36.

Editorial on Trinity Church. *AABN* 2 (17 February 1877): 49–50.

"A Boston Basilica." *The Architect* 18 (28 April 1877): 274.

T. Sergeant Perry. "Colour Decoration in America." *The Architect* 18 (20 October 1877): 210–11.

Frederick Law Olmsted, Leopold Eidlitz, and Henry H. Richardson. *Report of the Advisory Board Relative to the Plans of the New Capital.* Albany, 1877.

Consecration Services of Trinity Church, Boston, February 9, 1877; with the consecration sermon by Rev. A. H. Vinton, D. D., an historical sermon, by Rev. Phillips Brooks, and a description of the church edifice, by H. H. Richardson, architect. Boston, 1877. (See *AABN* 2 [11 August 1877]: 254, 258–59. Richardson's *Description* has been reprinted a number of times.)

1879

Henry Van Brunt. "The New Dispensation in Monumental Art." *Atlantic Monthly* 43 (May 1879): 633–41. (See *AABN* 5 [24 May 1879]: 164–65. Reprinted in William A. Coles, *Architecture and Society: Selected Essays of Henry Van Brunt,* 135–44. Cambridge, Mass., 1969.)

Montgomery Schuyler. "The Capitol of New York." *Scribner's Monthly* 19 (December 1879): 161ff. (See *AABN* 6 [13 December 1879]: 185; [27 December]: 206–8; 9 [8 January 1881]: 13; 10 [29 October 1881]: 203–7.)

1881

Montgomery Schuyler. "Recent Building in New York III: Dwellings." *AABN* 9 (23 April 1881): 196–97.

"S.E." "The 'Brattle Square' Church." *AABN* 10 (8 October 1881): 165–66.

Talcott Williams. "A Brief Object-Lesson In Springfield Architecture." *AABN* 10 (12 November 1881): 227–31.

1882

Clarence Cook. "Architecture in America." *The North American Review* 135 (September 1882): 243–52.

1883

"Modern American Architecture." *British Architect* 19 (5 January 1883). (See correction, 30 March, 154–55.)

Address of Charles Francis Adams, Jr. and Proceedings at the Dedication of the Crane Memorial Hall, at Quincy, Mass., May 30, 1882. Cambridge, Mass., 1883.

Oakes Ames: A Memoir with an Account of the Dedication of the Oakes Ames Memorial Hall at North Easton, Mass., November 17, 1881. Cambridge, Mass., 1883.

1884

"Studio and Office of Mr. H. H. Richardson, Architect, Brookline, Mass." *AABN* 16 (27 December 1884): 304.

H. H. Richardson. *Description of Drawings for the New County Buildings for Allegheny County, Penn.* Boston, 1884.

1885

E. W. Lightner. "A Glimpse of Some Washington Homes." *Harper's New Monthly Magazine* 70 (December 1884–May 1885): 520–33.

M. G. Van Rensselaer. "Recent Architecture in America." *Century Magazine* 6–10 (May 1884–October 1886): 548–58, 676–87.

"The County Buildings at Pittsburgh." *Harper's Weekly* 29 (28 February 1885): 141–42.

"The Best Ten Buildings in the United States." *AABN* 17 (13 June 1885): 282.

"Our Cincinnati Letter." *Building, an Architectural Monthly* 3 (July 1885): 110.

"Cincinnati Chamber of Commerce. . . ." *Building, an Architectural Monthly* 3 (August 1885): 126.

"Austin Hall, Harvard Law Schools. . . ." *Builder* 49 (19 December 1885): 858.

H. H. Richardson. *Austin Hall, Harvard Law School, Cambridge, Mass.* Monographs of American Architecture, 1. Boston, 1885 (and 1886). (See review, *AABN* 17 [16 May 1885]: 233.)

[H. H. Richardson.] *Cincinnati Chamber of Commerce,* Boston, [1885].

1886

Selected obituaries:

Boston Evening Transcript, 28 April 1886, 8.

New York Sun, 28 April 1886.
New York Times, 29 April 1886, 4.
Boston Evening Transcript, 30 April 1886, 5.
Peter B. Wight. *Inland Architect* 7 (May 1886): 59–61.
[Clarence Cook.] *The Studio* (New York) 1 (1 May 1886): 264–65.
AABN 19 (1 May 1886): 205–6.
"L. H. W." [Herbert Langford Warren?] *The New York Star,* 2 May 1886, 2.
Architect 35 (21 May 1886): 306–7.
Building News 50 (21 May 1886): 817–18.
Builder 50 (22 May 1886): 740.
Karl Hinckeldeyn. *Zentralblatt der Bauverwaltung* 6 (5 June 1886): 221–22.
"M. C. S." *Scientific American*, August 1886: 21.

John B. Gass. "Some American Methods." *The Royal Institute of British Architects, Journal of Proceedings,* n.s. 2 (18 March 1886): 179–88.

———. "New York State Capitol, Albany." *Builder* 50 (17 April 1886): 574.

"Those Who Will Complete Mr. Richardson's Buildings." *AABN* 19 (8 May 1886): 218.

"Buildings Designed by the Late H. H. Richardson, Architect." *AABN* 20 (11 September 1886): 122.

Phillips Brooks. "Henry Hobson Richardson." *Harvard Monthly* 3 (October 1886): 1–7. (Reprinted in P. Brooks, *Essays and Addresses,* 482ff. New York, 1894.)

"Some Incidents in the Life of H. H. Richardson." *AABN* 20 (23 October 1886): 198–99.

Henry Van Brunt. "Henry Hobson Richardson, Architect." *The Atlantic Monthly* 58 (November 1886): 685–93. (Reprinted in William A. Coles, ed., *Architecture and Society: Selected Essays of Henry Van Brunt,* 170–79. Cambridge, Mass., 1969.)

H. H. Richardson. *The Hoyt Public Library, East Saginaw, Michigan.* Boston, [1886].

H. H. Richardson. *The Ames Memorial Building[s], North Easton, Mass.* Monographs of American Architecture, 3. Boston, 1886.

George William Sheldon, ed. *Artistic Country Seats.* New York, 1886–87. (Reprinted 1979.)

1887

"Railway Stations at Wellesley Hills, Waban, Woodlands, Auburndale, Brighton, South Framingham, Palmer, Holyoke and North Easton, Mass." *AABN* 21 (2 February 1887): 103.

"The Late Mr. Richardson." *Royal Institute of British Architects, Journal of Proceedings,* n.s. 4 (9 February 1888): 141–42.

Alexander Graham. "Architecture in the United States." *Royal Institute of British Architects, Journal of Proceedings,* n.s. 4 (8 March 1888): 193–96.

C. H. Blackall. "Boston Sketches—The Churches." *The Inland Architect and News Record* 12 (December 1888): 77–78.

Alfred Waterhouse. "Waterhouse on Richardson." *AABN* 24 (1 December 1888): 253–54. (Originally published in the *Builder* 55 [10 November 1888]: 336–40.)

F. E. Wallis. "Wheel Sketches." *Building, An Architectural Weekly* 9 (6 October 1888): 107–8.

Phillips Brooks. "Henry Hobson Richardson." *Appleton's Cyclopedia of American Biography* (New York, 1888), 5: 241–42.

Mariana Griswold Schuyler Van Rensselaer. *Henry Hobson Richardson and His Works*. Boston, 1888 (Facsimile edition with introduction by James D. Van Trump, Park Forest, Ill., 1967. Facsimile edition in paperback with introduction by William Morgan, New York, 1969. Reviews in *AABN* 24 [7 July 1888]: 10–11, and *The Nation* 47 [2 August 1888]: 94–95).

Arthur H. Chester. *Trinity Church in the City of Boston: An Historical and Descriptive Account with a Guide to Its Windows and Paintings*. Cambridge, Mass., 1888.

Boston and Its Surroundings: A Guide Book. Boston, 1888.

H. H. Richardson. *Trinity Church, Boston*. Monographs of American Architecture, 5. Boston, 1888.

H. H. Richardson. *The Billings Library: The Gift to the University of Vermont of Frederick Billings*. Boston, ca. 1888.

1889

C. H. Blackall. "Boston Sketches—Business Buildings." *The Inland Architect and News Record* 12 (January 1889): 94–96.

Edward Atkinson. "Slow-Burning Construction." *The Century Magazine* 37 (February 1889): 566–79.

C. H. Blackall. "Boston Sketches—Suburban Work." *The Inland Architect and News Record* 13 (March 1889): 40–41; (April 1889): 53–54.

[C. S. Sargent?] "The Railroad-Station at Auburndale, Massachusetts." *Garden and Forest* 2 (13 March 1889): 124–25.

———. "The Railroad-Station at Chestnut Hill." *Garden and Forest* 2 (3 April 1889): 159–60.

William R. Cutter. "A Model Village Library." *New England Magazine*, n.s. 1 (September 1889–February 1890): 617–25.

A. R. Willard. "Recent Church Architecture in Boston." *New England Magazine* n.s. 1 (September 1889–February 1890): 641–62.

1891

Montgomery Schuyler. "Glimpses of Western Architecture: Chicago." *Harper's Magazine* 83 (August 1891): 395–406; (September 1891): 559–70. (Reprinted in M. Schuyler, *American Architecture*, New

York, 1891, and in M. Schuyler, *American Architecture and Other Writings,* edited by William H. Jordy, Jr., and Ralph Coe, 246–91, Cambridge, Mass., 1961.)

[F. L. Olmsted (or M. G. Van Rensselaer?)] "Architectural Fitness." *Garden and Forest* 4 (19 August 1891): 385–86. (Cited at length in S. B. Sutton, *Civilizing American Cities,* 13ff., Cambridge, 1971.)

Montgomery Schuyler. "An American Cathedral." In *American Architecture,* 86–111. New York, 1891. (Reprinted in M. Schuyler, *American Architecture and Other Writings,* edited by W. H. Jordy, Jr., and R. Coe, 229–45, Cambridge, 1961.)

———. "The Romanesque Revival in America." *Architectural Record* 1 (July 1891–July 1892): 151–98. (Excerpted in M. Schuyler, *American Architecture and Other Writings,* edited by W. H. Jordy, Jr., and R. Coe, 200–225, Cambridge, Mass., 1961.)

1892

Karl Hinkeldeyn. "Henry Richardson und seine Bedeutung für die amerikanische Architektur." *Deutsche Bauzeitung* 26 (6 February 1892): 64–66.

A. O. Elzner. "A Reminiscence of Richardson." *The Inland Architect and News Record* 20 (September 1892): 15.

1893

H. Langford Warren. "The Use and Abuse of Precedent." *Architectural Record* 2 (13 February 1893): 11–15; (3 April 1893): 21–25.

Robert D. Andrews. "The Broadest Use of Precedent." *Architectural Record* 2 (15 May 1893): 31–36.

Mariana Griswold Schuyler Van Rensselaer. *Art Out-of-Doors.* New York, 1893. (Reissued 1903.)

1894

Leopold Gmelin. "Architektonisches aus Nordamerika." *Deutsche Bauzeitung* 28 (15 September 1894): 453–56; (29 September 1894): 481–83; (3 October 1884): 485–87; (6 October 1894): 495–98; (20 October 1894): 520–22; (27 October 1894): 532–34; (17 November 1894): 566–70; (29 November 1894): 582–83.

Horace Townsend. "H. H. Richardson, Architect." *Magazine of Art* 17 (1894): 133–38.

Edward Hale. "H. H. Richardson and His Work." *New England Magazine,* n.s. 2 (December 1894): 513–32.

"First Baptist ('Brattle Square') Church, . . . Boston, Mass."*AABN* 43 (24 March 1894): 142.

1895

S. Bing. *La Culture artistique en Amérique*. Paris, 1895 (Reissued in translation as Samuel Bing, *Artistic America, Tiffany Glass, and Art Nouveau,* introduction by Robert Koch, Cambridge, Mass., 1970.)

1896

John B. Gass. "American Architecture and Architects, with Special Reference to the Works of the Late Richard Morris Hunt and Henry Hobson Richardson." *Journal of the Royal Institute of British Architects,* 3d ser. 3 (6 February 1896): 229–32.

A. D. F. Hamlin. *A Text-Book of the History of Architecture*. New York, 1896. (Several later eds.)

Russell Sturgis. "Shepley, Rutan & Coolidge." *Architectural Record* 6 (July–September 1896) (supplement).

1897

Paul Graef and Karl Hinkeldeyn. *Neubauten in Nordamerika*. Berlin, 1897 (2d, augmented, ed. 1905.)

Ashton R. Willard. "College Libraries in the United States." *New England Magazine,* n.s. 17 (September 1897–February 1898): 422ff.

1898

Richard Streiter. "Nordamerikanische Architektur." *Allgemeine Zeitung,* 6 June 1898, 4–7.

1899

Leopold Gmelin. "American Architecture from a German Point of View." *The Forum* 27 (August 1899): 690ff.

J. B. Noel Wyatt. "Modern Romanesque Architecture." *Architectural Review* (Boston) 6 (August 1899): 103–7.

Cuyler Reynolds. "The New York Capitol Building."*Architectural Record* 9 (October–December 1899): 142–57.

H. Langford Warren. *Picturesque and Architectural New England*. Boston, 1899.

1900

W. A. Langdon. "The Method of H. H. Richardson." *The Architect and Contract Reporter* (supplement to *The Architect and Building News,* London) 63 (9 March 1900): 156–58. (Also published as "On the Architect's Part in His Works. . . ." *Canadian Architect and Builder* 13 [February 1900].)

1901

Russell Sturgis. "H. H. Richardson." *A Dictionary of Architecture and Building* (New York, 1901–2), 3 cols. 291–92.

1902

O. Gruner, "Persönliche Erinnerungen an Henry Richardson." *Deutsche Bauhütte* 6 (17 July 1902): 228.

Joy Wheeler Dow. "American Renaissance." *Architects' and Builders' Magazine* 4 (November 1902): 66ff.; 5 (October 1903): 17ff. (Reissued as a book of the same title, New York, 1904.)

Charles M. Robinson. "A Railroad Beautiful." *House and Garden* 2 (1902): 564–70.

1903

Irene Sargent. "Trinity Church, Boston, as a Monument of American Art." *Craftsman* 3 (March 1903): 329–40.

1904

E. P. Overmire. "A Draftsman's Recollection of Boston." *The Western Architect* 3 (February 1904): 18–20, etc.

C. M. Robinson. "Surburban Station Grounds." *House and Garden* 5 (April 1904): 182–87.

1906

John Theodore Comes. "The Allegheny County Court House." *The International Studio* 28 (March–June 1906): iii–vii.

1910

F. Rudolf Vogel. *Das amerikanische Haus*. Berlin, 1910.

1911

William Wells Bosworth. "Mens Sana in Corpore Sano."*Architectural Record* 30 (August 1911): 151–64.

Montgomery Schuyler. "The Building of Pittsburgh, Part II: The Business Quarter and the Commercial Building." *Architectural Record* 30 (September 1911): 204–82.

1913

Royal Cortissoz. *Art and Common Sense*. New York, 1913.

The Reminiscences of Augustus Saint-Gaudens. Edited by Homer Saint-Gaudens. New York, 1913.

1914

J. H. Phillips. "The Evolution of the Suburban Station." *Architectural Record* 36 (August 1914): 122–27.

[The Cincinnati Astonomical Society.] *Richardson, the Architect and the Cincinnati Chamber of Commerce Building*. Cincinnati, 1914.

1917

A. D. F. Hamlin. "The American Country House." *Architectural Record* 42 (October 1917): 291–391.

The Boston Architectural Club Yearbook. Boston, 1917.

1920

"Alterations to the City Hall at Albany, N.Y." *The American Architect* 117 (30 June 1920): 809–15.

1924

Lewis Mumford. *Sticks and Stones*. New York, 1924. (Revised ed., 1955.)

1927

Charles A. Coolidge. "Henry Hobson Richardson." In *Later Years of the Saturday Club,* edited by M. A. DeWolfe Howe, 193–200. Boston and New York, 1927.

1929

Henry-Russell Hitchcock. *Modern Architecture*. New York, 1929.

1931

Glenn Brown. *1860–1930 Memories*. Washington, D.C., 1931.

Lewis Mumford. *The Brown Decades*. New York, 1931. (Reissued 1971.)

1933

Jeffery Brackett et al. *Trinity Church in the City of Boston, Mass.* Boston, 1933.

Thomas E. Tallmadge. "Holographs of Famous Architects." *American Architect* 143 (March 1933): 10–12.

1936

Ralph Adams Cram. *My Life in Architecture*. Boston, 1936.

[Henry-Russell Hitchcock.] *The Architecture of Henry Hobson Richardson Arranged by the Department of Architecture of the Museum of Modern Art*. New York, ca. 1936. Mimeograph.

Henry-Russell Hitchcock. *The Architecture of H. H. Richardson and His Times*. New York, 1936. (Revised ed., Hamden, Conn., 1961; paperback ed., Cambridge, Mass., 1966.)

1939

Walter Shepherd. "Von Herkomer's Folly." *Country Life* 86 (16 December 1939): 636.

1940

Buford Pickens. "H. H. Richardson and Basic Form Concepts in Modern Architecture." *The Art Quarterly* 3 (1940): 273–91.

1941

Sigfried Gideon. *Space, Time and Architecture*. Cambridge, 1941. (Several later eds.)

Lewis Mumford. *The South in Architecture*. New York, 1941. (Reprinted 1967.)

1943

Talbot F. Hamlin. "Henry Hobson Richardson." *Dictionary of American Biography*. New York, 1943.

1949

Kenneth J. Conant. *Tres conferencias sobre arquitectura moderna en los Estados Unidos*. Buenos Aires, 1949.

1950

Carson Webster. "Richardson's American Express Building." *JSAH* 9 (March 1950): 20–24.

Henry-Russell Hitchcock. "Richardson's American Express Building: A Note." *JSAH* 9 (March 1950): 25–30.

1951

Welles Bosworth. "I Knew H. H. Richardson." *Journal of the American Institute of Architects* 16 (September 1951): 115–27.

1952

Edgar D. Romig. *The Story of Trinity Church in the City of Boston*. Boston, [1952].

1953

Carroll L. V. Meeks. "Romanesque before Richardson in the United States." *The Art Bulletin* 25 (March 1953): 17–33.

Ernest Scheyer. "Henry Adams and Henry Hobson Richardson." *JSAH* 12 (March 1953): 7–12.

Fello Atkinson. "American Architecture Comes of Age." *Architects' Year Book* (London) 5 (1953): 123–32.

1955

"H. H. Richardson." *The Hall of American Artists*. New York, 1955. pp. 49–59.

Vincent J. Scully, Jr. *The Shingle Style: Architectural Theory and Design from Richardson to the Origins of Wright*. New Haven, 1955. (Revised ed. 1974.)

1956

"One Hundred Years of Significant Building." *Architectural Record* 120 (October 1956): 193; (December 1956): 178.

1957

James D. Van Trump. "The Romanesque Revival in Pittsburgh." *JSAH* 16 (October 1957): 22–29.

1958

J. D. Forbes. "Shepley, Bulfinch, Richardson and Abbott, Architects; An Introduction." *JSAH* 17 (Fall 1958): 19–31.

William S. Huff. "Richardson's Jail." *Western Pennsylvania Historical Magazine* 41 (1958): 41–59.

1959

Robert Koch. "American Influence Abroad, 1886 and Later." *JSAH* 18 (May 1959): 66–69.

1962

L. Draper Hill, Jr. *The Crane Library*. Quincy, Mass., 1962.

Richard H. Randall, Jr. *The Furniture of H. H. Richardson*. Boston, 1962.

1963

Richard H. Janson. "Mr. Billings' Richardson Library." *University of Vermont Alumni Magazine* (May 1963): 8–10.

1964

Cecil R. Roseberry. *Capitol Story*. Albany, 1964.

David T. Van Zanten. "H. H. Richardson's Glessner House, Chicago, 1886–1887." *JSAH* 23 (May 1964): 106–11.

1965

Charles Price. "Henry Hobson Richardson: Some Unpublished Drawings." *Perspecta* 9/10 (1965): 200–210.

Alfred Browning Parker. *You and Architecture*. New York, 1965.

1966

Leonard K. Eaton. "Richardson and Sullivan in Scandinavia." *Progressive Architecture* 47 (March 1966): 168–71.

H. R. Dieterich, Jr. "The Architecture of H. H. Richardson in Wyoming: A New Look at the Ames Monument." *Annals of Wyoming* 38 (April 1966): 49–53.

Larry J. Homolka. "Richardson's North Easton." *Architectural Forum* 124 (May 1966): 72–77.

Henry-Russell Hitchcock. *Richardson as a Victorian Architect*. Northampton, Mass., 1966.

1967

Marika Hausen. "Gesellus—Lindgren—Saarinen vid sekelskiftet." *Arkkitehti Arkitekten* (Finnish Architectural Review) 9 (September 1967): 6–12.

"Chicago School of Architecture Foundation." *Inland Architect*, n.s. 10 (May 1967): 12–13.

Bainbridge Bunting. *Houses of Boston's Back Bay*. Cambridge, Mass., 1967.

Sigmund A. Lavine. *Famous American Architects*. New York, 1967.

1968

J. William Rudd. "The Cincinnati Chamber of Commerce Building." *JSAH* 27 (May 1968): 115–23.

Walter Kidney. "Jove's Gentle Giant." *Progressive Architecture* 39 (June 1968): 168, 172, 182.

Theodore E. Stebbins, Jr. "Richardson and Trinity Church: The Evolution of a Building." *JSAH* 27 (December 1968): 281–98.

1969

[Museum of Fine Arts, Boston.] *Back Bay Boston: The City as a Work of Art.* Boston, 1969.

James F. O'Gorman. "Henry Hobson Richardson and Frank Lloyd Wright." *The Art Quarterly* 32 (Autumn 1969): 292–315.

[The Oakes Ames Memorial Hall Association and the Easton Historical Society.] *The Architecture of Henry Hobson Richardson in North Easton, Massachusetts.* Introduction by Robert F. Brown. North Easton, 1969.

1970

Dimitri Tselos. "Richardson's Influence on European Architecture." *JSAH* 29 (May 1970): 156–62.

A. W. Reinink. "American Influences on Late Nineteenth-Century Architecture in the Netherlands." *JSAH* 29 (May 1970): 163–74.

Marc Friedlaender. "Henry Hobson Richardson, Henry Adams, and John Hay." *JSAH* 29 (October 1970): 231–46.

Edgar Kaufmann, Jr., ed. *The Rise of an American Architecture.* New York, 1970.

Ernst Scheyer. *The Circle of Henry Adams: Art and Artists.* Detroit, 1970.

1972

Arnold Lewis. "Hinckeldeyn, Vogel, and American Architecture." *JSAH* 31 (December 1972): 276–90.

Leonard K. Eaton. *American Architecture Comes of Age: European Reaction to H. H. Richardson and Louis Sullivan.* Cambridge, Mass., 1972.

Albert Fein. *Frederick Law Olmsted and the American Environmental Tradition.* New York, 1972.

1973

James F. O'Gorman. "O. W. Norcross: Richardson's 'Master Builder.'" *JSAH* 32 (May 1973): 104–13.

Cynthia Zaitzevsky. "A New Richardson Building." *JSAH* 32 (May 1973): 164–66.

1974

James F. O'Gorman. "The Making of a 'Richardson Building.'" *Harvard Magazine* (October 1974): 20–29.

Helene Barbara Weinberg. "John La Farge and the Decoration of Trinity Church." *JSAH* 33 (December 1974): 323–53.

James F. O'Gorman. "Henry Hobson Richardson." *Encyclopaedia Britannica* (1974), 15: 828.

———. *Henry Hobson Richardson and His Office: Selected Drawings.* Cambridge, Mass., 1974.

Lawrence Wodehouse. "Henry Hobson Richardson's Home at Arrochar." *Bulletin of the Victorian Society in America* 2 (September 1974): 6.

1975

Myra Dickman Orth. "The Influence of the 'American Romanesque' in Australia." *JSAH* 34 (March 1975): 318.

Henry-Russell Hitchcock. "An Inventory of the Architectural Library of H. H. Richardson." *Nineteenth Century* 1 (January 1975): 27, 31; (April 1975): 18–19.

Malcolm M. Fleming. "The Saving of Henry Hobson Richardson's Union Station, New London, Connecticut." *American Art Review* 2 (July–August 1975): 29–40.

Arnold W. Klukas. "Henry Hobson Richardson's Designs for the Emmanuel Episcopal Church, Pittsburgh." *American Art Review* 2 (July–August 1975): 64–76.

1976

James F. O'Gorman. "A Tragic Circle." *Nineteenth Century* 2 (Autumn 1976): 46–49.

1977

Richard Chafee. "Richardson's Record at the Ecole des Beaux-Arts." *JSAH* 36 (October 1977): 175–88.

Franklin K. B. Toker. "Richardson 'en concours': The Pittsburgh Courthouse." *Carnegie Magazine* (November 1977): 13–29.

Robert F. Brown. "The Aesthetic Transformation of an Industrial Community." *Winterthur Portfolio* 12 (1977): 35–64.

Cynthia D. Kinnard. "The Life and Works of Mariana Griswold Van Rensselaer." Ph.D. dissertation, The Johns Hopkins University, 1977.

Melanie Simo, ed. *Henry Hobson Richardson: The Allegheny County Courthouse and Jail, Part I.* Pittsburgh, 1977.

1978

Henry-Russell Hitchcock. "French Influence on Nineteenth Century Architecture in the United States." *Architectural Design* 48 (1978): 80–83.

Francis R. Kowsky. "H. H. Richardson's Project for the Young Men's Association in Buffalo." *Niagara Frontier: Journal of the Buffalo and Erie County Historical Society* 35 (1978): 29–35.

James F. O'Gorman. "The Marshall Field Wholsale Store: Materials toward a Monograph." *JSAH* 37 (October 1978): 175–94.

———. "H. H. Richardson and the Architecture of the Commuter Railway Station." In *Around the Station: The Town and the Train* (Danforth Museum exhibition catalog), 19–34. Framingham, Mass., 1978.

Trinity Church: The Story of an Episcopal Parish in the City of Boston. Edited by Bettina A. Norton. Boston, 1978.

S. A. Kohler and Jeffrey R. Carson. *Sixteenth Street Architecture I.* Washington, D.C., 1978.

1979

James F. O'Gorman. "On Vacation with H. H. Richardson: Ten Letters from Europe, 1882." *Archives of American Art Journal* 19 (1979): 2–14.

Jack Quinan. "H. H. Richardson and the Boston Granite Tradition." *Little Journal of the S. A. H. Western New York Chapter* 3 (February 1979): 20–29.

Anne Farnam. "H. H. Richardson and A. H. Davenport: Architecture and Furniture as Big Business in America's Gilded Age." In *Tools and Technologies: America's Wooden Age,* edited by Paul B. Kebabian and William C. Lipke. Burlington, Vt., 1979.

1980

Francis R. Kowsky. "The William Dorsheimer House: A Reflection of French Suburban Architecture in the Early Work of H. H. Richardson." *The Art Bulletin* 62 (March 1980): 134–47.

Henry-Russell Hitchcock. "Henry Hobson Richardson's New York Senate Chamber Restored." *Nineteenth Century* 6 (Spring 1980): 44–47.

Ann J. Adams. "The Birth of a Style: Henry Hobson Richardson and the Competition Drawings for Trinity Church, Boston." *The Art Bulletin* 62 (September 1980): 409–33.

Suzanne Stephens. "Richardson on the Half Shell." *Progressive Architecture* 61 (November 1980): 92–95.

Francis R. Kowsky. *Buffalo Projects: H. H. Richardson.* Buffalo, N.Y., 1980.

Marian Page. *Furniture Designed by Architects.* New York and London, 1980.

1981

William Seale. "Glowing Revival for 'most beautiful room in America.'" *Smithsonian Magazine* (November 1981): 146–52.

John Russell. "Henry Hobson Richardson." In *Three Centuries of Notable American Architects,* edited by Joseph J. Thorndike, Jr., 110–29. New York, 1981.

Allegheny County Bureau of Cultural Affairs. *H. H. Richardson's Allegheny County Courthouse and Jail.* Pittsburgh, 1981.

J. P. Ribner. "H. H. Richardson and the Hotel Brunswick." *Marsyas* 21 (1981–82): 47–49.

1982

John Coolidge. "H. H. Richardson's Youth: Some Unpublished Documents." In *In Search of Modern Architecture: A Tribute to Henry-Russell Hitchcock,* edited by Helen Searing, 165–71. Cambridge, Mass., and London, 1982.

James F. O'Gorman. "Documentation: An 1886 Inventory of H. H. Richardson's Library, and Other Gleanings from Probate." *JSAH* 41 (May 1982): 150–55.

William H. Pierson, Jr. "H. H. Richardson." *Macmillan Encyclopedia of Architects* (New York, 1982), 3: 558–75.

Jeffrey Karl Ochsner. *H. H. Richardson: Complete Architectural Works.* Cambridge, 1982. (Paperback ed., with additions, 1984.)

1983

Margaret Henderson Floyd. "H. H. Richardson, Frederick Law Olmsted, and the House for Robert Treat Paine." *Winterthur Portfolio* 18 (Winter 1983): 227–48.

Bernice Loss. *Austin Hall after a Century.* Cambridge, 1983.

Andrew Saint, "Leviathan of Brookline," *Art History* 63 (September 1983): 376–79.

1984

Jeffrey Karl Oshsner. "H. H. Richardson's Frank William Andrews House." *JSAH* 43 (March 1984): 20–32.

1985

Bainbridge Bunting. *Harvard: An Architectural History.* Completed and edited by Margaret Henderson Floyd. Cambridge, Mass., 1985.

1986

James F. O'Gorman. "America and H. H. Richardson." In *American Architecture: Innovation and Tradition,* edited by D. G. DeLong, M. Searing, and R. A. M. Stern, 93–102. New York, 1986.

1987

James F. O'Gorman. "Man-Made Mountain: 'Gathering and Governing' in H. H. Richardson's Design for the Ames Monument in Wyoming." In *The Railroad in American Art: Representations of Technological Change,* edited by Susan Danly and Leo Marx. Cambridge, Mass., and London, 1987.

Note: James F. O'Gorman, "Richardson, Olmsted, and the Rejected Civil War Monuments for Worcester and Buffalo," In *Three Centuries / Two Continents: Essays . . . Honor of Robert C. Smith,* ed. K. L. Ames and N. H. Schless (Watkins Glen, N.Y.), is cited by Ochsner and others, but the festschrift was canceled and this article never published.

Source Notes

The discussion of Brookline in chapter 1 first appeared in *H. H. Richardson and His Office: Selected Drawings* (Cambridge, Mass.: Harvard College Library, 1974), 2–13.

Some of the material in chapter 2 was originally published in "H. H. Richardson and the Architecture of the Commuter Railway Station," in *Around the Station: The Town and the Train,* exhibition catalog published by the Danforth Museum (Framingham, Mass., 1978), 19–34.

Chapter 4 is a revised version of "The Marshall Field Wholesale Store," *Journal of the Society of Architectural Historians* 37 (October 1978) : 175–94; portions also appeared in "America and H. H. Richardson," in *American Architecture: Innovation and Tradition,* ed. D. De Long et al. (New York: Rizzoli, 1985).

Portions of chapter 5 appear in "America and H. H. Richardson," in *American Architecture: Innovations and Tradition,* ed. D. De Long et al. (New York: Rizzoli, 1985), and in "Man-Made Mountain: 'Gathering and Governing' in H. H. Richardson's Design for the Ames Monument in Wyoming," in *The Railroad in American Art: Representations of Technological Change,* ed. Susan Danly and Leo Marx (Cambridge, Mass.: MIT Press, 1987).

Chapter 6 is a revised version of "H. H. Richardson and the Architecture of the Commuter Railway Station," in *Around the Station: The Town and the Train,* exhibition catalog published by the Danforth Museum (Framingham, Mass., 1978), 19–34.

Portions of chapter 7 appeared in "Henry Hobson Richardson and Frank Lloyd Wright," *Art Quarterly* 22 (Autumn 1969) : 308–11.

Index